'6 Christopher Knight began his personal research to gate the origins of the Judao-Christian belief system and uals still used by Freemasons. His findings led to the pu _tion of his first book, *The Hiram Key* in 1996. Much to his surprise it was an immediate, international best seller – ar earing in 37 different languages. He has since written es of books that describe the findings of his ongoing ches.

n recent years, working with fellow researcher Alan Butler, stopher Knight has been able to demonstrate that many of ey elements of modern science are actually remnants of a highly sophisticated system of geometry and astronomy that dat from before the dawn of history. The utter improbability ounding these detailed discoveries forced him to question felong tendency towards atheism.

Outside of his historic researches and writing Christopher Kr ght is the CEO and Chairman of a leading international al and social media enterprise.

# GOD'S BLUEPRINT

## Scientific Evidence that Earth was Created for Humans

### Christopher Knight

WATKINS
Sharing Wisdom Since
1893

This edition published in the UK and USA 2015 by
Watkins, an imprint of Watkins Media Limited
19 Cecil Court
London WC2N 4HE

enquiries@watkinspublishing.co.uk

Design and typography copyright © Watkins Media Limited 2015

Text Copyright © Christopher Knight 2015

Artwork copyright © Watkins Media Limited 2015

Illustrations by Barking Dog Art, except images on pages 125 and 127
courtesy of the author

1 3 5 7 9 10 8 6 4 2

Typeset by JCS Publishing Services Ltd, www.jcs-publishing.co.uk

Printed and bound in Europe

A CIP record for this book is available from the British Library

ISBN: 978-1-78028-749-2

www.watkinspublishing.com

# CONTENTS

*Dedicated to my grandchildren:*
*Sam, Isabelle, Eli, Max, Toby, Betsy and Eleanor.*

*Every smile makes the world a better place.*

# ACKNOWLEDGEMENTS

Edmund Sixsmith, for his support, humour and
determination

Jim Russell, for his engineering insights

Gordon Freeman, for his open mind and generous
encouragement

Karl Pribram, for his astonishing insights

Alan Butler, for being my fellow traveller on a great
journey into the past

Fiona Spencer-Thomas, my tireless agent

Michael Mann, my publisher, who has been a great
supporter

Christopher Westhorp, a great editor with an eye for
every detail

My wife Caroline, for putting up with my unreasonable
working hours

# INTRODUCTION

This is not a book I could ever have imagined writing. I have no religious beliefs whatsoever and no desire to debate aspects of faith with anyone.

However, I have come down a winding pathway of personal research since 1976 that began with a simple question that has no apparent connection with the ultimate findings described in this book. I began by looking into the origins of the rituals used by Freemasonry, which led me to attempt to reconstruct the origins of ancient Judaism, which in turn led me to investigate prehistoric astronomy.

Unlikely as it may seem, these rather anodyne subjects have opened a doorway on the past that has taken me deeper and deeper into the nature of our planet and the universe itself. Century by century rolled back, and I was eventually to find myself taken deep into prehistory. I had expected the rituals used by Freemasons to be a 16th- or 17th-century invention, but as my investigation delved further back in time the inescapable evidence emerged that Freemasonry is a memory-strand connected to a prehistoric science based upon astronomy and the measuring of the world to an accuracy that is way beyond modern comprehension.

Some casual readers, intrigued by the title, may have just switched off. A preconception that Freemasonry is esoteric nonsense or some kind of secretive élite will have overtaken any open-mindedness. This is understandable, but anyone who appreciates hard evidence and is relaxed about challenging his or her prejudices will be amazed at the story I have to tell.

This more recent period of my research was conducted with my good friend and colleague Alan Butler, who began his own research trying to understand a curious Minoan artefact known as the Phaistos Disc. This small double-sided clay disc from the island of Crete, dating from the second millennium BC, is covered with undecipherable hieroglyphs. Alan deduced that it was, possibly, and among other things, a stunningly accurate perpetual calendar. He wasn't sure why at the time, but he contacted me because he felt that his research was in some way connected to my own investigations.

We spent several years working together, and this led to the reconstruction of an ancient super-science of breath-taking accuracy and complexity. We published several books together, explaining our findings, which became progressively more and more mathematically testable. Whilst most of history and much of archaeology is about opinion and the interpretation of physical artefacts, Alan and I were faced with hard, verifiable forensic evidence from a time before writing existed anywhere in the world. Before the rise of the ancient Egyptian, the Sumerian, the Vedic or the Chinese civilizations, the world had possessed a comprehensive system of measurement that is the origin of all the units in use today.

Introduction

We invited a number of archaeologists to check out our
findings, but they are not generally trained to understand
astronomy or mathematics. One high-profile archaeologist
who is supposed to be astronomically competent was initially
positive, responding that he had greatly enjoyed my previous
book *Uriel's Machine*, which opened up the subject. Then
he suddenly refused to respond to correspondence, despite
having said that we appeared to be onto something very
important.

However, when we put the evidence in front of
experts from other academic fields – including astronomy,
engineering, statistics, physics and chemistry – we were told
that our findings were robust, even if our techniques are a
little home-cooked. One friend, with a medical degree and
an MSc in mathematics, was very surprised when she ran
through our findings. Dr Hilary Newbegin said that she was
stunned by our findings concerning the Sun–Earth–Moon
relationship, which occurs with no other planets in our solar
system.

But as things progressed to the next stage I became
more and more troubled. Slowly, it became obvious that the
beautiful, integrated system of measures from the extremely
distant past was much more than a way of describing the planet
upon which we live. It transpires that this super-science was
not an abstract invention: it went way beyond the boundaries
of the Earth and apparently reveals a complete plan – and any
plan has a predetermined, intended outcome. However much
my agnostic brain sought for other conclusions, there was
recurring pressure to consider that this was God's blueprint
for building everything – everything that has led to advanced
life on Earth!

And the plan appears to be on public display. We seem to be invited to participate.

It is the premise of this book that there is now an entirely new class of evidence to bring to the God debate. Faith and prophecy aside, there is a new, complementary, way of considering theology. Based on engineering principles and planetary metrology, I believe we are being given a glimpse of the great plan. I can only call it 'God's Blueprint'.

The bottom line is: if there is indeed a blueprint for an engineering project, there must be an intended outcome. And it seems highly probable that there is a message from the Maker contained within the very fabric of this plan. Could we humans be on the verge of a new relationship with the Great Architect of the Universe?

# IMPORTANT DEFINITIONS USED IN THIS BOOK

This book is not about religion. It does not challenge anyone's beliefs, nor does it support or question the scriptures of any faith. It is about science and evidence that intelligent atheists and open-minded people of faith should consider with equal enthusiasm.

The sole purpose of this small book is to present dramatic new evidence that changes the nature of the 'God debate'. It appears that life on Earth was deliberately planned and is not the result of mindless cosmic happenstance.

Those who have religious faith, or those who believe only in the principles of science, will not find anything in these pages that will disturb them. But because of the emotive nature of the subject matter, it is essential to establish at the outset what is meant by certain terms used in these pages.

## God
The consciousness that (may have) created the universe and all of its rules.

There are four kinds of argument for His – or Her – existence: cosmological, teleological (the 'design argument'), ontological and Pascal's 'wager'. The cosmological and teleological arguments appeal to certain facts about the world. The cosmological argument holds that the very existence of the universe needs explanation and the only adequate explanation is that it was created by an original and deliberate cause. The teleological argument is also called the argument from design, and specifically singles out the intricacy of nature as key evidence for God's existence. The ontological argument suggests that God's existence can be proven purely from reflection on the concept of God itself. In the ontological argument no facts about the world are required. Pascal's 'wager' is an argument that it is in your best interest to believe in God's existence on the basis that it costs nothing, but the consequences of not believing, and being wrong, are terrible.

## Religion
One of a large number of organized belief systems that, through cultural narratives, symbols, traditions and sacred histories, provide a shared perception of a deity (or deities) and, usually, a framework of morality, ethics and laws. Religious frameworks tend to provide a meaning to life for adherents and frequently give an explanation for the existence of humankind and the visible universe.

The world's major religions are highly structured with clerical hierarchies, clear requirements for adherence (including regular meetings for the purposes of veneration of their deity) and designated holy locations and written scriptures. Religions, past and current, have provided a social framework with festivals, feast days and rites of passage, as well as prayer, sacred songs, music, art and dance forms.

Most religions teach that God (singular or multifaceted) is not only the creator of the universe, but He (normally a male) has a personal relationship with each believer. This communication is either directly through prayer or comes via a conduit in the form of a priestly hierarchy; this is the case with the Roman Catholic Church in which the pope is the Earthly conduit to God.

## Faith

Religious faith is a belief in a transcendent reality beyond the range of normal physical experience. The reality of God is implied by intellectual and emotional deduction by believers rather than proven in a scientific manner by virtue of the five physical senses.

Membership of a formal faith normally involves an acceptance that a set of teachings concerning humankind's relationship with a deity is factually true, without the requirement for any supporting evidence. Historical scriptures are taken as being literal accounts of past events and predicted futures are considered to be preordained certainties. Because 'faith' is not dependent upon testable evidence it is not possible to prove or disprove beliefs. People with faith frequently suggest that scientists who are also atheists are unduly focused on the issue of 'how?' and uninterested in the concept of 'why?'

## Spirituality

Intellectual contemplation of nature and the individual's place within it. Spirituality is a reflective and usually sensitive

xvii

outlook on existence that can arise from involvement with a
formal religious belief system or it can be a highly developed
set of entirely personal values. As such, spirituality can exist
without any reference to God or otherworldliness.

## Mysticism

This is a form of spirituality that often expresses itself in
organized movements: Christian monastic orders, Kabbalism
and Hassidic Judaism, and the numerous Sufi brotherhoods
in Islam. In Hinduism, ascetics (often practitioners of yoga)
seek *moksha* or 'liberation' from the world. Mystics seek,
through meditation or ascetic practices, to become identified
with God, who is understood to dwell within them. Thus,
Hindu mystics will say, 'I am Brahman', just as the famous
Muslim mystic, Mansur al-Hallaj (executed 922) was known
for the heretical exclamation *Ana'l-Haqq* or 'I am the Truth'
(that is, the Godhead).

## Agnosticism

Agnosticism is an openness to the possibility of the existence
of a God but a rejection of organized religion, and particularly
the metaphysical claims within scriptures. In essence the
agnostic is a 'floating voter' who sees a difference between
belief and knowledge, but does not reject the possibility of
the existence of God or some form of higher purpose for the
universe. Within agnosticism there are two principal groups:
'agnostic atheists' (those who do not believe that a deity exists,
but do not deny it as a possibility) and 'agnostic theists' (who
believe that some kind of God does exist, but do not accept
that any religious belief system is authentic).

## Atheism

Atheism is the belief that the universe, and everything in it, exists due to natural and random forces without any purpose or preordained destiny. The concept of God is rejected as irrational and unnecessary, and adherents of religion are considered to be people driven by superstition. For many atheists the belief in a benevolent, omnipotent God is inconsistent with the level of human suffering seen in the world, and the idea of a creator God cannot provide a solution to the origins of the universe because it simply raises the question, 'Who made God?'

## Science

The word 'science' is from Latin *scientia*, meaning 'knowledge'. It is a systematic enterprise that builds and organizes knowledge in the form of testable explanations and predictions about the universe. A scientific theory is empirical and is always open to falsification if new evidence is presented. That is, no theory can ever be considered certain as science is based on the concept of fallibilism. A scientific method seeks to explain the events of nature in a reproducible way, and to use these findings to make useful predictions. This is done through observation of natural phenomena, and experimentation that simulates natural events. A scientific method allows for highly creative problem solving whilst minimizing any effects of subjective bias on the part of its users.

## Creation

The zero point in time and space when everything replaced nothing. There is a scientific consensus that the universe, as we observe it, is around 13.7 billion years old. It is widely thought to have emerged from a single point in what is termed the Big Bang, although some astrophysicists believe that there have been many such events.

There are primitive (pre-science) descriptions of the origins of humans and all of nature in the scriptures of various world religions. A substantial number of people, particularly in the United States of America (USA), believe that the account given in the Christian Old Testament is historical fact, having been revealed by God to the Hebrews in the Middle East during the first and second millennia BC. Many fundamentalists date the beginning of everything as being just a few thousand years ago.

Conversely, Hinduism has scriptures describing multiple creations occurring over trillions of billions of years.

The great Muslim mystic Shaykh Muhyi'l-Din Ibn al-'Arabi (d 1240) argued in *Fusus al-Hikam*, 'The Bezels of Wisdom', that the entirety of creation shrinks to a single point and reappears from the point repeatedly, and so quickly no human being can notice the difference. Everything in creation is an effulgence (*tajalli*) of God.

# Chapter 1

# THE IMPROBABILITY OF EXISTENCE

'I think, therefore I am.'

*René Descartes*

How odd. Creation kicks off with a spectacular cosmic Big Bang and then after 13.7 billion years of personal oblivion you suddenly became self-aware. Then you soon come to realize that within a handful of decades you will be gone again – for all eternity. You may be little more than a speck of recycled stardust in a universe of unimaginable hugeness, but you are YOU – the very centre of everything.

But why? Why of all the countless galaxies, stars and planets, and of all the creatures that ever lived on Earth, are you here now – sensing, watching, thinking, experiencing joy and sadness, and probably astonished wonderment? Why do I exist and what is the purpose of the universe if we can only experience it for such a brief time?

Probably since hominids first stood up straight and gazed at the world around and above them, the questions they asked were: Where did everything come from? How come I'm alive to see this? Did someone or something make this all happen?

Many people do not concern themselves with such apparently unanswerable questions. Others turn to philosophy or religion, and increasingly large numbers expect science to give them some glimpse of what it all could mean.

We humans are robust creatures. Despite the fact that we are little more than animated bags of water hanging on a mineral frame, we can withstand difficult conditions and even survive without food for many weeks. It is apparently thanks to eons of beneficial evolution that we are perfectly designed for our environment. Almost 99 per cent of the mass of the human body is made up of the six elements oxygen, carbon, hydrogen, nitrogen, calcium and phosphorus. Another 0.85 per cent is composed of five other elements: potassium, sulphur, sodium, chlorine and magnesium, plus a few trace elements – all of which are essential to life.

Whatever we are made of does not describe the reality of the essence of what it means to be human.

Every human is special. We differ from other creatures because we are able to define ourselves by our own self-awareness, resulting in a situation where there is a simple polarity to the universe. We all know that 'there is me and then there is everything else'. Each and every one of us is an emotional–intellectual island connected to that 'everything else' by the complex interpretation of stimulus to our five senses.

Two small regions of our skin have developed the ability to detect the movements of photons and transmit impulses to our brains, where they are decoded to give us the magic of sight. Eyes first appeared during the early Cambrian period about 540 million years ago when there was a rapid explosion of life on Earth. Two other apertures on either side of our brains make sense of a cacophony of colliding compression waves in the gases of our atmosphere to give us hearing. Then we have skin sensitive enough to inform us about shape and texture, a mouth that in the form of taste accurately differentiates between different chemical substances we are about to consume, and we have an air inlet that can pick out the presence of a specific molecule within a million others in the atmosphere.

These five connection modes cause us to have interaction with the 'everything else', especially other humans – so we do not exist alone. These points of stimulus combine to give life to the most remarkable array of aspects of self. Love, fear, loathing, compassion, laughter and countless other emotions make us special and mark us out as entities that are utterly different to the rest of creation. But how and why have we become so spectacularly differentiated from other combinations of recycled stardust? What makes Neil Armstrong more special than the 3.5-billion-year-old rock he first lifted from the lunar surface?

## Can science explain existence?

Science is surely the greatest idea that ever happened in the universe. It is a method of enquiry that removes dependence of thought from the hubris of priesthoods and the ramblings of charlatans and replaces it with testable, shareable facts. The rigorous logic that underpins the scientific method has driven reason for several centuries, creating a pool of understanding that has brought about our modern, technologically based world. Without doubt, science provides a framework for the organization of observations in a mutually meaningful way that minimizes the likelihood of mistake or delusion.

Science is also self-repairing. According to Thomas Kuhn, in his groundbreaking study, *The Structure of Scientific Revolutions*, ideas that have become sclerotic and are no longer yielding dividends become conventional and are defended by the older generation of scientists in a given field. But the younger generation shows itself willing to opt for change and thus introduces a paradigm shift, as when Nicolaus Copernicus challenged the beliefs of his day and declared the Earth moved round the Sun. Paradigm shift after paradigm shift has successfully moved science forward, despite a human tendency to cling to established theory.

The problem for everyday science – and the issues we have been dealing with – is one of demarcation: deciding what is real science and what is not; what has practical outcomes and what is simply metaphysics. This problem preoccupied the early thinking of an Austrian philosopher of science, Karl Popper (1902–94), in later life Sir Karl Popper, who is widely considered to have been one of the greatest thinkers of the 20th century. Popper wanted to know how to differentiate between hard science and matters such as Marxism or Freudian psychoanalysis, both of which claimed the status of scientific disciplines. He knew that these and other theoretical structures offered valuable insights into history or the workings of the human mind, but he was unsure how to treat them in practice. He later abandoned his fascination with Marxism and wrote a study of totalitarianism, both communist and fascist, which remains a classic to this day.

Popper was aware that scientists had always worked backwards. They used (and many still use) inductive reasoning: making observations, carrying out experiments based on those observations, then developing broad theories. But Popper could see that observations are never pure, since they are preceded by existing theories, by the experience of the observer and by a host of other influences, distortions and assumptions that often lead to false ideas.

An example of this often given by Popper is the now-outdated belief that all swans are white. Based on observation, the statement seems unchallengeable. But the moment someone spotted a black swan in Australia, the original observation was shown to be quite false. In this way, even a small observation that sheds new light on something may be enough to overthrow centuries of scientific assumptions.

There can be no doubt; science is wonderful. It makes sense of what we experience and provides explanations to satisfy the naturally inquisitive human mind. However, it is less than intuitive when the questions move to the most fundamental levels of existence. Quantum physics has demonstrated that human logic does not apply in the world of sub-atomic particles, where information appears to traverse the entire universe in no time at all and a cat can be mathematically proven to be both alive and dead at the same time. Not only that, but in quantum theory, all parts of the universe, however distant they might seem to be from one another, are actually very close and can make an impact on one another across what are, in conventional physics, immeasurable distances.

What appears to be simple and straightforward is not so easy if we had the ability to look closer at solid objects. Pick up a large pebble on the beach and tap it on your head. You soon realize that it is best to do it gently because that solid lump of rock will hurt or even kill you if too much power is used.

But if we were able to peer into that pebble we would see that it conforms to the rules laid down by quantum mechanics. The solid rock is made up of something like 1,000 trillion, trillion atoms, each of which is composed of smaller sub-atomic particles, called protons and neutrons – and they in turn are built of quarks – and electrons. But most of that heavy pebble is simply empty space. If an atom were scaled up so that its nucleus was the size of the Earth, the distance to its closest electrons would be two and a half times the distance between the Earth and the Sun. In between there is nothing at all.

It is quite wonderful that we can know such information about the nature of our world. But the question has to be asked: whilst science may be the most powerful intellectual tool that we humans possess, can it ever provide a complete explanation for the existence we all perceive? Consider the following 'facts' – which are now accepted by all mainstream physicists: the total electrical charge of the universe is precisely zero; the rotation of the universe is nil; and, amazingly, it appears that the total energy of everything boils down to exactly zilch, a big fat zero – plus or minus nothing at all.

'The bottom line is', says leading physicist, Peter Atkins, 'that the initial endowment of energy at the creation was exactly zero, and the total energy has remained fixed at that value for all time.'* This leads Atkins, and a large number of

* Atkins, P, *On Being: A scientist's exploration of the great questions of existence*, Oxford University Press, Oxford, 2011

similarly minded scientists, to deduce that our lives are but a transient blip of awareness in a cauldron of meaningless chaos that began with nothing and will end with nothing.

If this is true, and it seems it is, then science has to be of secondary importance to philosophy. Surely our primary task has to be to intellectually explain our existence in some other way than simply seeking to describe the traits of the matter we think we are made of.

## Is science a new religion?

The term 'scientist' is used a great deal, yet it is less than two centuries old. It was first coined by an Anglican priest and leading theologian by the name of William Whewell. By general usage a scientist is someone who is involved in research at a university, a government department or in industry. Some practitioners such as medical doctors and lecturers also consider themselves to be scientists but they are only such insofar as they follow the principles of scientific deduction.

Science is not a new infallible scripture, where we are slowly learning more and more about everything until we eventually will reach a point of perfect all-knowingness. The reality is that new findings can turn yesterday's scientific facts into today's falsities, as in Kuhn's paradigm shifts. That the scientific community lives with a permanent preparedness to change its mind, even wholesale change, marks it out as intellectually superior to other 'carved-in-stone' belief systems.

Where religions have their prophets and saints, science has its heroes who are admired for their curiosity, their insights and ultimately their proofs. Yet even the most respected scientists are likely to be proven wrong in some aspects of their work. This is something that does not happen very often in the intellectually frozen world of scriptures. At least that is the way that science is supposed to work. Sometimes, perhaps often, individuals fall short of the objectivity that they claim. Despite increasing evidence that certain alternative medical systems like homeopathy, herbalism and acupuncture may well be effective, the mainstream medical community persists in dismissing them with greater scorn than scientific interest. As the eminent physician and opera director Jonathan Miller once commented in a television debate with homeopaths (themselves all doctors), 'Even if you could prove to me that what you say is true, I still wouldn't be interested.'

I have no personal interest whatsoever in homeopathy and I do not know whether it works at all, but I have observed that members of the medical establishment will frequently cite that there is no evidence to support the claims made for homeopathy. By this they mean controlled blind trials and peer-reviewed papers. The problem is that these objections are, in themselves, frequently unscientific. The trials they refer to were designed for the administering of chemical or biological substances that have a broadly similar effect on the physiological functioning of everyone.

All homeopaths (many being practising physicians) state that a homeopathic remedy is entirely individual for each patient, rather than being a universal chemical action, as is the case for modern drug therapy. As such, experiments with identical potions being administered to groups of people simply would not work. And, as homeopathy is distilled water with a claimed trace memory, it is impossible to give a placebo, which is the basis of the standard blind trial.

If homeopathy does bring meaningful medical benefit to individuals, as claimed by its supporters, its efficacy will have to be assessed by means that are compatible with its supposed performance profile. To complain that it has not passed a test designed for other products is about as daft as complaining that a bicycle has not passed an airworthiness test.

Another complaint frequently voiced against homeopathy is that it is an affront to common sense to argue that a substance can be medically beneficial after being repeatedly diluted in water until no single molecule of the original remains. Surely, critics state, it is obvious that pure distilled water is exactly that, no mater what it once contained – and it is ridiculous to suggest that this water can cure any ailment.

It is certainly true to claim that the premise of homeopathy is counterintuitive. But so are other aspects of the world around us. Quantum physics is based on completely unreasonable assumptions if we apply the logic of our daily lives. How can it be that there are particles that have to revolve through 720° to return to their original orientation? That this does happen is fully accepted as a reality by modern physicists.

I have no idea whether or not homeopathy has any medical benefit at all, or, if it has, whether its function is physical or psychological. What I would observe, though, is that there are a lot of scientifically trained people who are not being scientific when discussing the matter. In behaving in this way they are treating science as a religion – whereby the tenets laid out by the 'priesthood' are the truth and must be protected from the blasphemy of the deniers.

Science is not a cosy, cause-and-effect rulebook, as was once assumed, and anyone who loves science must be prepared to be shocked. Had Isaac Newton been able to meet Albert Einstein and learned about relativity he would have been stunned but, being a great scientist, surely he would have embraced the new knowledge with open arms?

Science will never fail to surprise anyone who understands that it is merely a means of us humans making sense of the universe – however improbable our observations and resulting deductions may become.

Whilst most physicists agree that everything adds up to zero, others also argue that you can get something out of nothing – but only when an object is moving very close to the speed of light. As such, 'creation' must be an ongoing thing, rather than a one-off event 13.7 billion years ago.

It turns out that even 'empty space' is far from empty, because it contains huge numbers of particles that pop in and out of existence following the strange laws of quantum mechanics, which require that even a perfect vacuum must have fluctuations of pairs of short-lived particles. These virtual particles, usually particles of light (photons), have been proved to exist in experiments known as the 'Casimir effect', but now Chris Wilson and his team at Chalmers University of Technology in Gothenburg, Sweden, have gone a step further by actually pulling pairs of photons out of a void and launching them into our 'real' world.

Where in all of creation do these particles belong? Or are they nothing to do with our universe as we know it?

It would seem that these brain-stressing conclusions mean that scientists may never, through observation and deduction alone, be able to explain the most fundamental questions about reality. At some point surely even the most super-rational scientist has to admit that there is a role for the philosopher – or even the theologian?

So, whilst science is undoubtedly based on much more solid ground than popular religions, it does seem to be mired in pretty much the same issues of 'why' rather than the relatively easy 'how'. As such, the gap between the God and no-God lobbies is arguably not as great as some people might suspect. Perhaps we could call this observation-based, fundamental philosophy of 'why', the scientific-theological model.

## Chapter 2

# WHERE DID EVERYTHING COME FROM?

'All difficult things have their origin in that which is easy,
and great things in that which is small.'

*Laozi*

Taking this scientific-theological point of view for a moment, let us consider the possibility that the beginning of the cosmos was a conscious act conducted by a designer – let's call it God – with complete control over events. Having the ultimate 'blank sheet of paper' upon which to write, God has the freedom to create the infinite number of rules that will pervade and govern His new universe. Our stunningly clever scientists of the 20th and 21st centuries have been able to stare deep into the night sky and reverse-engineer events in the early moments of creation to establish with some certainty that this event occurred a period of time ago equal to 13.7 billion current Earth orbits of the Sun.

According to the Big Bang theory, within an unimaginably tiny sliver of time ($10^{-37}$ seconds) from the beginning of time-space, nothingness became a singularity that immediately grew exponentially. This initial inflation of the universe consisted of elementary particles and temperatures so high that the random motions of particle–antiparticle pairs of all kinds were continuously being created and destroyed in collisions. Within the blink of an eye a very small excess of quarks and leptons over antiquarks and antileptons resulted in a dominance of matter over antimatter and the fundamental forces of physics and the parameters of elementary particles were in place.

Next, after about 379,000 years the electrons and nuclei began to combine into atoms – mostly hydrogen. Then, slowly over a longer period of time, gravity meant that the ever-so-slightly denser regions attracted nearby matter and grew even denser – forming gas clouds – and then became stars and formed galaxies.

Many people assume that the Big Bang theory is proven fact but it's actually just the most popular theory around today. Astrophysicist George F R Ellis has pointed out that the Big Bang is little more than a good suggestion. He has said: 'People need to be aware that there is a range of models that could explain the observations… For instance, I can construct you a spherically symmetrical universe with Earth at its centre, and you cannot disprove it based on observations… You can only exclude it on philosophical grounds. In my view there is absolutely nothing wrong in that. What I want to bring into the open is the fact that we are using philosophical criteria in choosing our models. A lot of cosmology tries to hide that.'*

---

* Gibbs, W, 'Profile: George F. R. Ellis, thinking globally, acting universally', *Scientific American*, October 1995, vol 273, no 4, p 55

The theory of the Big Bang is another arena within the world of science that has generated a great deal of bad feeling towards anyone who does not comply with the convention.

Halton Arp, an award-winning American astronomer and protégé of Edwin Hubble, was surprised when he was attacked by fellow scientists after he dared to question the Big Bang theory of the universe. Arp was eventually forced to pursue his studies in exile.

Arp had been a staff astronomer at the Mount Wilson and Palomar Observatories in California for almost 30 years, where he appeared to accept the consensus view of the beginning of the universe. One of the key pieces of evidence that gave rise to the theory is the apparent ongoing expansion of the universe. The light from distant objects indicates their movement by shifts in its spectrum, analogous to the increase in pitch of a locomotive as it approaches and then a drop in pitch when it has passed you.

This Doppler shift, as it is known, means that a star approaching the observer would emit light waves compressed or 'shifted' towards the blue end of the spectrum, since blue is at the high-frequency end of the visible spectrum; likewise, if a star is moving away from the observer, any light waves it emits get stretched and are 'redshifted', red being at the low-frequency end of the spectrum. It was noted by astronomers that light from other galaxies is redshifted, and therefore all the galaxies in the universe must be moving away from us, and furthermore the most distant ones are moving away from us at the greatest rate. This led astronomers to presume that this was the Big Bang happening as they watched.

During the 1960s, however, astronomers began to discover intense radio sources whose spectra are shifted dramatically towards longer, redder wavelengths of light, implying they are moving away from us at enormous velocities and must be extremely distant. Arp began looking at these quasars, as they became known, and noticed that many appeared to be lying quite close in the sky to galaxies, often in alignment with them. Then in 1971 he claimed to have found a 'bridge' of gas joining a galaxy named NGC 4319 and a quasar that sits next to it in the sky. As this quasar had a far higher redshift than the galaxy, according to conventional Big Bang theory it should have been billions of light years further away. The apparent proximity simply did not fit with the ideas of the day.

Most cosmologists dismissed the issue by assuming that Arp had made a mistake simply because the two objects were in the same line of sight. Arp responded to this criticism by producing many more images of other linked deep space objects, yet with very different redshifts. One showed a quasar-like object that had a redshift which placed it about a billion light years from Earth, yet appeared to be in front of a galaxy only 70 million light years away.

Arp went on to suggest that quasars are created in and ejected by galaxies, and have an 'intrinsic' high redshift that has nothing to do with distance or velocity.

Arp found himself among a small band of astronomers who proposed a rival theory to the Big Bang, known as Steady State, which had first been proposed by Hermann Bondi and Thomas Gold, and was further developed by Fred Hoyle. Steady State holds that the universe has always looked much the same and, if it is expanding, new matter must be created to maintain its general appearance.

Whilst the Big Bang theory is still the most popular explanation for the origin of the universe, it is still only a theory and the whole debate remains open. Despite this, Arp found himself being treated as a pariah. In the early 1980s he was told that his research was going nowhere and the committee that allocated time on the major astronomical telescopes he used informed him that he could 'no longer make those kinds of investigations'.

## Could creation be just a happy accident?

Is God really necessary to explain the existence of the universe? The short answer is probably no – but even leading scientists have always found it is remarkably difficult to argue the cosmic-accident stance.

If we go back to the early days of modern science, Isaac Newton, one of the most respected scientific minds of the 17th century, saw God as the masterful creator whose existence could not be denied in the face of the grandeur of all creation. Newton explained that his own investigations into the laws of nature were simply a means to get closer to the mind of God. As the man who first described the force of gravity, he believed that it existed due to continual divine action. He wrote: 'Gravity explains the motions of the planets, but it cannot explain who set the planets in motion. God governs all things and knows all that is or can be done.'

The rules of physics, as we understand them to be today, begin to manifest in the very early period after the first creation of matter. These rules did not have to be as they are, yet had they been even very slightly different, the outcome would have been a swimming, chaotic soup of strange matter. The tiniest difference in the strength of gravity, the masses of all electrons, the number of spatial dimensions and many other factors would change everything. Had things not unfolded in exactly the way they did there would be no structured cosmos at all.

Physicists are agreed. The starting point for the rule-book of the universe was a miracle beyond all imaginable miracles. Quite simply, it should not have unfolded in the way it did.

Of particular importance to us mortals is the precision of the fine-tuning of the laws of physics relating to carbon, the element on which all known life is based. According to the Big Bang theory, the original creative event produced hydrogen and helium, but no carbon at all. So the big question is, where did the all-important carbon in our bodies come from? Physicists have concluded that most of the chemical elements heavier than helium were manufactured due to the nuclear fusion in the centre of stars – but that still does not explain the existence of carbon.

The answer came from Sir Fred Hoyle, the famous University of Cambridge astronomer who, as previously mentioned, had been a supporter of the Steady State theory. He observed that carbon could only have been formed from the simultaneous collision of three helium nuclei. However, Hoyle pointed out that the chances of any three helium nuclei coming together at the same point in time and space is ridiculously unlikely given their tiny size and the vastness of empty space around them. It is rather like three riflemen spread out in a circle half a mile apart from each other and firing into the air so that all three bullets collide together at the same moment. They have to get the timing perfect, as well as the direction and height. And that is assuming that all three bullets had exactly the same amount of explosive energy released as the trigger was pulled!

Given the vanishingly small probability of any carbon existing in the universe, Hoyle reasoned that a special factor must be at work to explain the abundance of this life-forming element.

Hoyle, working with Willy Fowler, a nuclear physicist at the California Institute of Technology, was able to demonstrate that carbon has a resonant state at exactly the right energy level to enable stars to manufacture it. However, this carbon resonance was itself dependent on the strength of the force that binds protons and neutrons together in the nucleus. If the strength of the force that determined the carbon resonance had been even the tiniest bit stronger or weaker, then we humans would not be here.

Fred Hoyle became troubled at the precise nature of the laws of physics and the consequential multiple layers of improbability of life occurring. He famously dismissed the accidental origin to life, saying: 'A junkyard contains all the bits and pieces of a Boeing-747, dismembered and in disarray. A whirlwind happens to blow through the yard. What is the chance that after its passage a fully assembled 747, ready to fly, will be found standing there?'

Hoyle's aircraft analogy made the point that it is very hard to believe that the laws of physics occurred randomly.

Hoyle was also the man who coined the term 'Big Bang' – but he used it as a term of derision, believing that a spontaneous explosion of nothingness could not explain everything. As a scientist, he concluded that the only reasonable explanation for the existence of intelligent life was that the organization of the cosmos must be controlled by some 'superintelligence' that guides its evolution through quantum processes. He observed: 'A common sense interpretation of the facts suggests that a superintellect has monkeyed with physics, as well as with chemistry and biology, and that there are no blind forces worth speaking about in nature. The numbers one calculates from the facts seem to me so overwhelming as to put this conclusion almost beyond question.'

Hoyle was well aware that his observations would not go down well among his peers, but he was not a man to be easily intimidated. In 1982 he presented 'Evolution from Space' for the Royal Institution's Omni Lecture in London, in which he said: 'If one proceeds directly and straightforwardly in this matter, without being deflected by a fear of incurring the wrath of scientific opinion, one arrives at the conclusion that biomaterials with their amazing measure or order must be the outcome of *intelligent design*. No other possibility I have been able to think of in pondering this issue over quite a long time seems to me to have anything like as high a possibility of being true.'

Sir Fred Hoyle was not in any way religious. Hoyle was reportedly an atheist during most of his early life but became agnostic as he realized that life was not a cosmological accident. It seems likely that Hoyle would have made little or no connection between his scientific observations, regarding an intellect behind creation, and any form of theology. However, that may be due to the difference in starting point rather than the end point.

# Chapter 3

# IS RELIGION RATIONAL?

'Science without religion is lame, religion without
science is blind.'

*Albert Einstein*

For many people, it is hard to conceive of a cosmic master-intellect in anything but the most abstract of terms. Throughout history, monotheists, Hindus, pagans and others have perceived of their deity (or deities) in intensely personal terms. This deity is understood as a transcendent being who communicates with human beings through scriptures, visions, trance states, or the medium of prophets, divine manifestations, priests or mystics like the Sufi *pir* or the Indian *guru*. This personal divinity is also approached through ritual (such as the Catholic Mass), pilgrimage, meditation, private and public prayer, some forms of asceticism, dance (as in the whirling of the Mevlevi dervishes of Anatolia), chanting, singing and even prolonged silence (as in Quaker meetings). Abstract notions of a superintelligence are not conventional in monotheistic religions and are largely the result of the impact of modern physics, including quantum physics, and astronomy. In themselves, such notions are more likely to remain intellectual than personal or inward. In that respect, the emergence of an intergalactic superbeing is unlikely to replace the inwardness of traditional piety, or the Quranic verse that describes God as being 'closer than your jugular vein'.

There is, it seems, plenty of room to have a healthy philosophical debate as to whether God created the universe – without necessarily becoming unscientific. However, there is another aspect to most religious people's view of God that is quite separate from the question of creation. And that is His assumed current connection with humans in general and even a direct relationship with each individual.

Intellectual believers may well argue that it is rational to conclude that reality can be no more than the sum of all the parts of what can be observed, measured and tested. For them there are other issues to consider alongside day-to-day rationalism. Where does love fit in? Why do music, poetry and the visual arts have the ability to impact on the human psyche, creating hard-to-define states such as happiness, sadness or anger?

The ultra-rational scientist will dismiss such thoughts as simplistic and unnecessarily romantic. For them it is all quite mechanistic. The sound waves from the orchestra playing Mozart hit the eardrum, and photons bouncing off a Leonardo de Vinci painting enter the optic nerve via the eyeball, and all are received as signals that the brain processes into thoughts that might trigger hormones that are then sensed as emotions. This electro-chemical processing within the brain can be described by science; ergo, the emotions are considered to have been dealt with: a ticked box. For many technically minded people, further attempts at more abstract analysis are simply metaphysics.

Yet it is undeniable that religious belief is a highly intellectual idea. Whilst some believers proclaim the most bizarre histories, full of magic and otherworldly ideas, others are deeply philosophical and thought-provoking. However, in today's supposedly rational world, religious belief has fragmented so much it is difficult to consider theology as a single subject.

Some people will believe almost anything, however bizarre, without feeling the need for a single shred of what an average person would deem to be real evidence. Scientology – with its science fiction theories concerning the universe, alien beings and the human mind – falls readily into this category.

Science fiction author L Ron Hubbard established his new 'religion' in 1953 when he incorporated the Church of Scientology in Camden, New Jersey. Scientology teaches that people are immortal spiritual beings who have forgotten their true nature. The story of this faith deals with a dictator called Xenu who led the 'Galactic Confederacy' 75 million years ago. Xenu is said to have brought billions of his alien people to Earth (then known as 'Teegeeack') in spacecraft and housed them around volcanoes, before killing them with hydrogen bombs. Official Scientology scriptures hold that the essences of these many people have remained, and that they form around human beings in modern times, causing them spiritual harm.

With its use of popular 1950s imagery of the impending nuclear war and a near future of giant spacecraft, this new faith was a modern take on traditional myth development that has been used down the ages. Whilst it lacked any historical provenance, its absence of logic did not stop many people becoming attracted to it. Scientology even appealed strongly to some Hollywood stars, such as Tom Cruise and John Travolta. Cruise did not need any factual evidence to embrace this assumed history of the world. He is quoted as saying: 'There was a time I went through [the Scientology doctrine], I said, you know what, when I read it, I just thought "Woah", this is it. This is exactly it.'

Evidence formed no part of Cruise's decision that this was a revealed truth. Arguably this is no different to people who uncritically adopt beliefs they were born to. Can it be said that the claims for Xenu are any less likely than Moses meeting Yahweh on Mount Sinai or Jesus Christ feeding 5,000 people with a handful of loaves and fishes?

Whilst some people are predisposed to believe anything that suits them, however much the storyline collides with the apparent rules of the universe, others don't believe anything outside what they were taught at university. 'If it's not in my textbook it isn't true.'

Unlike the arts and humanities, science and medicine are taught via textbooks, and deviation from received wisdom is a sure path to failure for any questioning and argumentative students. Whereas students in subjects like philosophy or literature are actively encouraged to disagree with their teachers and question their authority, medics and physicists are discouraged from doing the same. The chief exception to this rule may be found in the Jewish world, where rigorous questioning and disagreement are the order of the day. Citizens serving in the Israel Defense Forces are encouraged to challenge officers, and one result is the astonishing level of innovation in Israeli IT, which is driven by a culture of improvement through direct criticism and rational debate. This stands in direct contrast to the state of affairs in most Muslim countries, where open debate is still discouraged and historic tradition is accorded respect – perhaps too much so. The desire to follow the teaching of the past has perhaps stifled the present, as any form of questioning, whether religious or political, can be met with often severe punishments. The result is frequently a failure to meet the challenges and needs of the modern world – something the Pakistani physicist Pervez Hoodbhoy has pointed out many times in clear and certain terms. He reports that 46 Muslim countries contributed 1.17 per cent of the world's scientific literature, whereas 1.66 per cent came from India alone and 1.48 per cent from Spain.*

There is no question that Islam has led the world in innovative thinking in the past, but it has not been as successful as some other religions in adjusting to an evolving world where science has to have the freedom to question the assumptions of earlier generations. The gap between religion and science did indeed seem to expand in the mid-20th century but there is reason to believe that there has been a distinct closing of the gap in more recent times. Even Stephen Hawking, the famous theoretical physicist and director of research at the Centre for Theoretical Cosmology at the University of Cambridge has softened his atheist stance somewhat, saying: 'The whole history of science has been the gradual realization that events do not happen in an arbitrary manner but that they reflect a certain underlying order, which may or may not be divinely inspired.'

---

* Hoodbhoy, Pervez, 'Science and the Islamic World – The quest for rapprochement', *Physics Today*, August 2007

# How old is God?

Reflective self-awareness is the essence of what might be called advanced intelligence. A bird may have the reasoning power to drop stones into a beaker of water to raise the water level so it can reach a floating morsel of food, but is this a demonstration of advanced intelligence? I suggest not.

It seems improbable that any creature other than humans has felt the need to contemplate the complexity of its own existence. We cannot know this for sure, but from the available evidence it appears unlikely that creatures which, technically, can be classified as intelligent would ever wonder why things happen. This ability to consider 'why' must have led humans to contemplate the existence of unseen forces that caused good and bad things to happen. This externalization of causation gave rise to the concept of the deity.

So, how far back in human history did people discover God? It seems probable that such a moment would have occurred at the same time as other forms of abstract thinking – such as painting, sculpture, self-adornment (with woad, and other things), singing, dancing, jewellery and contemplation of the beautiful.

It used to be thought that a 'creative explosion' around 40,000 years ago marked the beginning of a paradigm shift in cognitive sophistication. An apparently sudden proliferation of artworks across Europe suggested a watershed moment in human evolution. In 1989 the distinguished anthropologist Jared Diamond summed up the general view of this period by suggesting that humans were little more than 'glorified baboons' prior to this 'great leap forward'.

However, this seems to be at odds with the widely accepted theory that the human brain was fully developed well over 100,000 years ago. How come humans had the 'hardware' – a fully physiologically formed brain – yet no 'software' to generate sophisticated thinking?

This question caused many experts to doubt the Eurocentric 'cognitive leap' theory, but there was no hard evidence to support a counter-theory. Recently the time frame for creative thinking in terms of art and symbolism has been pushed back – so far back that it seems probable that it even predates the arrival of our own species, *Homo sapiens*. In the early 1980s, researchers in Israel discovered a Berekhat Ram figurine that resembles the c30,000-year-old 'Venus' figurines found in Europe – except that this was an astonishing 230,000 years old! The carving was crude, but microscopic analysis detected what was taken to be deliberate sculpting. This dating would mean this piece of artwork was the work of *Homo erectus* – a species that predates our own.

Some academics go further, such as a team of researchers led by Johan Lind at Stockholm University. In a paper published in 2013, Lind's team reported that they had looked at data on a human gene designated FOXP2, which is thought to be associated with linguistic development and changes in the vocal tract. Combining this with archaeological clues, for factors such as the use of fire and complex tools that gave rise to symbolism, they estimated that the modern mind could have developed as far back as 500,000 years ago. Lind stated: 'Things seen as uniquely human traits are deep in the phylogeny [the evolutionary tree of life].'

Many experts now consider that the capacity for abstract thought had arisen long before our ancestors left Africa, which suggests that non-tangible forces (gods) may have arisen at this early stage.

## Is there something beyond the rational?

The great religions of the world can be loosely divided into two groups: the largest is the Abrahamic, followed by those emanating from the Indian subcontinent.

In September 1999 I was invited to deliver the John D. Mackay Memorial Lecture at the Orkney Science Festival on the subject of detailed astronomical calculations contained within an ancient Jewish text known as the Book of Enoch and their apparent correspondence with archaeological artefacts in the British Isles. One evening over dinner I had the good fortune to talk with an elderly gentleman by the name of Karl Pribram, who was at the festival to speak about his work on quantum holography and the human brain.

Karl Pribram was in his eightieth year back then, and 14 years later at the time I am writing he is still an active professor at Georgetown University, an emeritus professor of psychology and psychiatry at Stanford University and a distinguished professor at Radford University. He was also professor at Yale University for ten years and at Stanford University for 30 years.

As a young man in World War Two he had been a neurosurgeon, and later became well known for his pioneering work on the definition of the limbic system and his ongoing neurological research into memory, emotion, motivation and consciousness.

The conversation that evening was truly amazing. Whilst the work that Karl is involved with is highly specialized, he was very good at turning complex ideas into something that a layperson like me could follow.

He explained how a generation earlier his peers had been coming to believe that they were starting to get a useful understanding of how the brain works, and it looked as though its functions would, in time, be described as an electro-chemical computer of some kind. But then the model started to look shaky. In Karl's words, 'Everything we thought we knew turned out to be wrong.'

Karl then really surprised me by saying: 'Every time we made a new discovery we found that it wasn't new at all.' He explained how this new understanding of how the brain works had been described in the distant past by the people of ancient India. Hindu traditions, it appeared, were correct in scientific detail.

The ancient Hindu texts known as the Vedas (meaning 'Knowledge') and the Upanishads, oral traditions said to contain revealed truths concerning the nature of ultimate reality, are very modern in their thinking.

It is claimed that matter is composed of infinitesimal particles called *bhutatmas*, which are described as the smallest units of consciousness. In Kashmir, the Shaivist school of philosophy, which is based on the Vedas, holds that matter is composed of *tattvas* – units of consciousness that are also a type of energy. Furthermore, there are many layers of consciousness in this system, where the densest forms refer to matter.

Karl Pribram has successfully demonstrated that the memory of the human being is not contained only in the brain, but rather that it is distributed through the surrounding space, not necessarily in the immediate vicinity of the person, in a similar way to a hologram. This means that the memories are held in a complete manner, even when the matter holding them is broken down – so if a small piece was cut out of a hologram, that fragment would still contain all of the information in the original hologram.

This is rather similar to the way that the DNA contained in the cells of a human liver, for example, not only contains the information required to make that specific organ, it also has all of the instructions to build the entire person.

When Pribram first published his insight into the way memory functions, he effectively rewrote the prevailing views of consciousness, which had always been based on the idea that memories resided at identifiable and precise locations within the physical brain.

Naturally, not everyone wanted to accept this radical new view and some academics attempted to disprove Pribram's results by cutting out various chunks of the brains of laboratory rats, which had previously been trained to run through complex mazes. They reasoned that if they chopped out the appropriate part of the rat's brain it would lose its memory of how to pass through the maze. This would then prove that the rat's memory was entirely contained within neurological tissue.

All of these attempts to disprove Pribram's hypothesis by partially lobotomizing laboratory rats failed. The rats continued to run effortlessly through the mazes that they had previously learned.

Some researchers were so outraged by their initial failure that they took more and more sections of brain out of their subjects. Much to the amazement of the team, the rats were not only able to walk, they could also pass through the maze.

The Bohm–Pribram holographic model of memory had to be accepted as hard science.

By its nature a hologram exhibits some very profound properties beyond the three-dimensionality of the image. It is actually the most profound means to distribute information throughout a given medium (including the brain). All of the information held is distributed over the entire image surface.

When Pribram first heard about holography, he felt he had found the missing link to the workings of the brain. Just as every portion of a piece of holographic film contains all the information necessary to create a whole image, every part of the brain holds all of the information necessary to recall an entire memory.

At first Pribram considered the holographic model of the brain to be an analogy but he came to realize that is a true hologramic function. This was the solution to the puzzle of how our brains manage to store so many memories in such a small space. John von Neumann, one of the greatest physicists of the 20th century, once calculated that over the course of the average human lifetime, the brain stores around $2.8 \times 10^{20}$ bits of information. This equates to around 800 bits for every second in the entire history of the universe from the supposed Big Bang to today.

A colleague of Karl Pribram, David Bohm, had suggested that were we to view the cosmos without the lenses of our telescopes, the universe would appear to us as a hologram. Pribram went further by suggesting that were we humans deprived of the 'lenses' of our eyes and our other sensory receptors, we would become immersed in holographic experiences.

This profound concept might explain a great deal about our past – and potentially shape our future.

## Sense and sensibility

If, as Karl Pribram suggests, our senses have become possibly too heightened and sophisticated, then we might be losing some aspect of our souls to the onslaught of practical information that swamps our lives today. Could we be blinded by the light and deafened by the cacophony of sounds that surround us?

Multitasking has become the norm. Listening to the TV commentator reading the news whilst looking at sports headlines floating across the screen – and simultaneously posting an update on a social media site via a tablet? Meaning is everywhere – trivial or serious; we have to be asleep to switch off these days.

Is this why Buddhist monks seek out trance states, whereby their five otherwise dominant senses are wound down? Is this why more 'primitive' societies, such as the Aboriginal Australians, sometimes seem to be more connected to the essence of our planet? And might this explain why animals have abilities that we do not share?

Before giant waves slammed into the coastlines of Sri Lanka and India due to the great tsunami of December 2004, wild and domestic animals seemed to know what was about to happen and fled to high ground. Hundreds of eyewitnesses reported that dogs refused to go outdoors, flamingos abandoned their low-lying breeding areas and zoo animals rushed into their shelters and could not be enticed back out.

The massive tsunami had been triggered by a magnitude 9 earthquake off the coast of northern Sumatra on 26 December causing the sea level to rise and rush as a moving slab across the Indian Ocean. The human death toll was massive but relatively few animals were killed, creating speculation that animals somehow knew about the impending disaster.

In Yala National Park on the west coast of Sri Lanka, the destruction was severe, yet all the elephants, leopards, deer and other wild animals managed to survive the event. H D Ratnayake, deputy director of the Sri Lanka Wildlife Conservation Society, said afterwards: 'I haven't seen any effects on the animals. They all escaped.' Asked to explain the survival of the animals, he replied by saying: 'They had a feeling ...'

There were countless similar accounts, such as one from Khao Lak, Thailand, where agitated elephants somehow knew the tsunami was coming. Their sensitivity saved the lives of many foreign tourists. Even the elephant handlers were amazed at the way that their animals behaved – 'I was surprised because the elephants had never cried before,' said mahout Dang Salangam. The elephants had started trumpeting in a way which Dang and his wife Kulada said could only be described as 'crying at first light', at about the same moment that the massive earthquake cracked open the seabed. There was apparently no time for vibrations to be carried through the ground, the sea or the air. The elephants soon calmed, but began wailing again an hour later, and this time they could not be comforted. 'They just kept running for the hill,' said Wit Aniwat, who works with the elephants. Those with tourists on their backs turned and headed for the jungle on raised ground behind the resort beach where at least 3,800 people were to die a short time later.

## Switching off to connect

If it is true that experts in meditation, more primitive peoples and animals have an ability to become 'aware' by some means beyond the normal senses, what chance is there for people who live in the noisy Westernized world of the 21st century? There is, it seems, at least one way of switching off the senses that may open up an otherwise closed pathway to somewhere unknown.

A sensory deprivation tank (SDT) is a temperature-regulated, saltwater-filled, soundproof and lightproof tank that can isolate its occupant from numerous forms of sensory input all at once. They were first devised in 1954 by neuroscientist John C Lilly when he decided to find out what your brain does when it's all alone for a while.

Today such SDTs contain water saturated with Epsom salts, which makes the water so dense that the subject floats with their entire body resting at its surface.

If you were to enter a SDT you would find that there is no light – so no sense of vision – and you would experience such total silence that you will be able to hear your muscles tense, your heart beat, and even your eyelids close. The extreme buoyancy of the water lends your environment a quality of almost zero gravity, with no sense of touch. The controlled body temperature warmth plays with your ability to perceive where your body ends and where the water and air begin.

But then what happens? What do people experience whilst they're in such a tank?

The answer is highly personalized. As with the claims for homeopathy, there is no mass effect that replicates in the same way with everyone. Some subjects describe hallucinations, heightened levels of introspection and the sensation that the mind has left the body. Even renowned physicist Richard Feynman described having hallucinations and out-of-body experiences whilst using sensory depravation tanks. These reports are very similar to those from people with extensive experience in meditation, and both practices have been linked to decreased alpha waves and increased theta waves in the brain – patterns most typically found in sleeping states.

One SDT subject reported that after some minutes he suddenly felt his feet start to sink and head start to rise. He moved his body to stop this, but immediately realized that his body was not actually moving. With a little practice he found that he could spin around in all directions – without actually having moved any physical part of his body. He said that he felt like a weightless, disembodied brain as he began having visual dreams. These were typically centred around flying or being a ship on the ocean with moonlight shining on him.

Whether or not modern life is a hindrance to certain primitive functions that could have considerable value, we generally take too much of our hi-tech lives for granted. We should perhaps reflect on just how wildly improbable our lives actually are.

# Chapter 4

# GLASS, RUBBER AND GASOLINE

'There are improbable things suspended in
space – like the Earth.'

*Meryl Streep*

The world is filled with highly improbable things that we
usually just accept as obvious and normal. Most people today,
including many scientists, appear to believe that if we can
describe something or simply give it a name, then we can
understand it. We use phenomena such as alternating current
electricity and radio waves to great effect, and we can describe
their various properties in great detail – but do we really
understand what they are and why they need to exist at all?
We know that in their chaotic form they are fundamental to
the universe, and if they did not exist the marvels of the 20th
century would not have happened.

Scientists acknowledge that there is an almost endless
list of improbable circumstances that conspired with great
exactitude to give rise to human existence. If any one of these

critical factors were not just as it is we would not exist. As we have seen, even the tiniest shift in the rules applying in our corner of the universe would have prevented you and the rest of us sentient beings from having originated in the first place.

This infinitely large improbability issue is normally explained away by something called the Anthropic Principle. This states that all of the improbable factors that led to our existence are a necessity because living observers would not be able to observe the universe were these laws and constants not constituted precisely in this way. Put succinctly, it amounts to the simple thought that everything has to be as it is or we wouldn't be here to see it.

But this seems to be a circular argument. In what way is this 'scientific' logic any more helpful than the theist claim that God designed everything?

The Anthropic Principle has been criticized by some people as being more of a philosophical argument than a scientific one. It arose after a number of observations indicated just how vanishingly small our chances of being here at all really were. One of the earliest of these 'problem' observations was made in 1961 when Robert Dicke of Princeton University realized that the age of the universe as seen by living observers cannot be random. Instead, he argued, biological factors constrain the universe to be in a 'golden age', neither too young nor too old. If the universe were just one tenth as old as its present age, there would not have been sufficient time to build up appreciable levels of metallicity (levels of elements above and beyond hydrogen and helium). Most importantly, of course, carbon – the basis of all known life – would not exist and small rocky planets would not exist. Conversely, if the universe was significantly older than it actually is, most stars would have turned into white dwarfs, and stable planetary systems would have already come to an end.

Dicke later reasoned that the density of matter in the universe must be almost exactly the critical density needed to prevent the Big Crunch – everything rushing to a single, massively dense point in space. However, if the cosmological constant were more than about ten times its observed value, the universe would suffer catastrophic inflation, which would preclude the formation of stars, and hence life. Furthermore, the observed values of the dimensionless physical constants governing the four fundamental interactions are balanced as if they were fine-tuned to permit the formation of commonly found matter and subsequently the emergence of life.

Even a slight increase in the strong nuclear force would bind the dineutron and the diproton, and nuclear fusion would have converted all hydrogen in the early universe to helium. This would mean that water and the long-lived stable stars essential for the emergence of life would not exist.

The Anthropic Principle had to be created as a 'more rational', and therefore supposedly scientific, escape route in logic to avoid having to consider God. Putting aside the improbability of life itself and our own personal existence, let us look at some more trivial aspects of our everyday lives.

Consider for a moment one very common object that we all take completely for granted: the car. It is estimated that in 2012 there were some 660,000,000 cars in the world and a new car rolls off a production line somewhere on the planet every 0.8 seconds, 24 hours a day.

The car transformed the industrialized world in the last century by bringing personal transportation to the masses.

Whilst people often lived and died in an area of a few tens of square miles in all previous generations, 20th-century men and women were increasingly able to travel widely as and when they chose.

Few people stop to ponder how amazing it is that machines like this work at all. An internal combustion engine typically produces over 100 controlled explosions every second with metal parts pushing and turning at fantastic speeds. They are truly remarkable, and only familiarity makes them seem unsurprising.

Cars are largely made of metal; a substance that in some form or other has been used by humans for around 11,000 years, and even steel has been in use for over 3,000 years. The rest of the vehicle is mostly glass, rubber and plastic, possibly with a few organic materials such as wood or leather on upscale variants.

The steel from which cars are made is basically rock. Pure metallic iron is virtually unknown on the surface of the Earth except as iron-nickel alloys from meteorites and very rare forms of deep mantle xenoliths. Therefore, all sources of commercial iron come from iron oxide minerals, the primary form being hematite, a mineral that is coloured black to silver-grey, brown or red. Iron ores consist of oxygen and iron atoms bonded together into molecules. To be converted to metallic iron it must be smelted to remove the oxygen. Oxygen–iron bonds are strong, and to remove the oxygen from the iron, a stronger elemental bond must be presented to attach to the oxygen. Carbon is used because the strength of a carbon–oxygen bond is greater than that of the iron–oxygen bond at high temperatures. The iron ore must therefore be powdered and mixed with coke, to be burnt in the smelting process.

So, metal is not too difficult to understand, but glass is remarkable. It is made of heated sand (silica), which is the most abundant mineral in the Earth's crust. The fact that it makes sheets of totally transparent material is a very happy coincidence because, without it, cars would have no windscreen or other windows to protect the occupants from wind, rain, snow or sandstorms. More fundamentally, driving on modern highways would be very dangerous as we would not have rear-view mirrors to monitor what is happening behind us. We could have a highly polished metal sheet to reflect images for us but they would be very poor quality compared to the perfection of glass. In the past, mirrors were indeed made of polished metal. The pure mirror reflects a frequent mystical trope in which physical things function as the mirrors of things in the invisible realm or attributes of the Godhead, something given great prominence in the *Fusus al-Hikam* of the Andalusian mystic Ibn al-'Arabi, referred to earlier.

Rubber exhibits unique physical and chemical properties that make it perfect for tyres and other important parts of the car, such as windscreen wipers. This rather miraculous substance was originally derived from latex, a milky colloid found in the sap of some plants – most particularly, the rubber tree. The plants are 'tapped' by making an incision into the bark of the tree and the sap collected is refined into a usable rubber. The purified form of natural rubber is the chemical polyisoprene, which is now also produced synthetically. It is estimated that 27 million tons of rubber were consumed in 2013.

The rubber tree initially grew in South America, where it had been used by the Olmec culture, which centuries later passed on the knowledge to the ancient Mayans, who boiled the harvested latex to make balls for sport. It was eventually seen by Charles Marie de La Condamine and he brought samples back to France in 1736.

Had such plants not delivered up such an extraordinary substance, cars could not have existed. Although there are now synthetic rubbers, they would not have been invented if the demand for motor car tyres had not grown so massively in the early 20th century. And, like the plastics so important in car manufacture, synthetic rubber is a derivative of the oil industry.

The relatively cheap availability of petroleum as a fuel for our cars has been central to the huge growth of personal transport in the last century. Had we not found oilfields across the globe, cars would have remained toys for the very rich, perhaps powered by vegetable oils or electricity. So, why do oil deposits exist?

As every child knows from their schooling, petroleum is a fossil fuel, having an organic origin such as colossal amounts of dead zooplankton and algae that accumulated on the ocean floor tens of millions of years ago. Children are taught that through various unknown geochemical processes across millions of years this material was converted to the mineral oil that we seek out and extract today. What they are not told is that this is a rather loose theory – an attempt to explain why this strange material exists on our planet. It most certainly is not proven fact.

It is hard to image how such vast volumes of living creatures could congregate into mile-high residues to await compression without decaying to nothing. Certainly, any inability to visualize such an extraordinary process will be dismissed as irrelevant by most geologists. But not all geologists by any means.

A small but highly respected number of experts do not accept the organic origin theory, and instead promote the 'abiogenic petroleum origin hypothesis', which maintains that hydrocarbons within Earth's interior are of an entirely inorganic origin. Chemists Marcellin Berthelot and Dmitri Mendeleev, as well as polymath astronomer Thomas Gold, championed the theory in the Western world by supporting the work done by Nikolai Kudryavtsev and Vladimir Porfiriev in the 1950s. It is currently supported primarily by Jack F Kenney, Vladilen Krayushkin and Vladimir Kutcherov.

Thomas Gold was a brilliant scientist and very original thinker. Whilst most academics stick tightly to the prescribed boundaries of their discipline and confine their thinking to the established dogmas of the times, Gold loved ideas. And he was not frightened to rock the academic boat. He first became interested in the origins of petroleum back in the 1950s, when he engaged in discussions on the matter with fellow astronomer Sir Fred Hoyle. But it was in the late 1970s, when the USA faced a major energy crisis, that Gold aggressively moved his work on petroleum forward again.

Gold reasoned that since petroleum and its component hydrocarbons were present across the entire universe, it was inherently odd to casually assume that on Earth they must be biological in origin. He noted how earthquakes facilitated the migration of methane gas from the deep Earth to the surface, leading him to speculate that any large earthquake would fracture the ground, opening up an escape route for gas once trapped deep inside the planet's core. Gold believed that this would explain the number of unusual phenomena associated with earthquakes, such as fires, flares, earthquake lights and gas emissions. With his colleague Steven Soter, Gold constructed a map of the world depicting major oil-producing regions and areas with historical seismic activity. Several oil-rich regions, such as Alaska, Texas, the Caribbean, Mexico, Venezuela, the Persian Gulf, the Urals, Siberia and Southeast Asia, were found to be lying on major earthquake belts. Gold and Soter concluded that these belts may explain the upward migration of gases through the ground and, subsequently, the creation of oil and gas fields.

Soon after Gold started publishing his theories, researchers discovered a number of ecosystems functioning under conditions of heat and pressure once thought impossible to sustain life. Another important piece of evidence that supported Gold's hypothesis was the known fact that some exhausted oil wells appeared to refill from nowhere, generating huge amounts of 'new' crude oil. All of this led Gold to propose that the Earth may possess at least 500 million years' worth of so-called 'fossil fuels'.

After conducting a range of major experiments, Gold eventually consolidated his theory in his 1992 paper 'The Deep Hot Biosphere' in the *Proceedings of the National Academy of Sciences of the United States of America (PNAS)*. Gold suggested that coal and crude oil deposits have their origins in natural gas flows that feed bacteria living at extreme depths under the surface of the Earth; in other words, oil is produced through tectonic forces, rather than from the decomposition of dead organisms. At the beginning of the paper, Gold also referred to hydrothermal vents that had recently been discovered pumping bacteria from the depth of the Earth to emerge on the ocean floor. He also noted that geologic structures where oil is found all correspond to 'deep Earth' formations, not the haphazard depositions found with sedimentary rock, associated fossils or even current surface life.

Gold pointed out that oil extracted from varying depths from the same oil field have the same chemistry – oil chemistry does not vary as fossils do with increasing depth. Also interesting is the fact that oil is found in huge quantities among geographic formations where quantities of prehistoric life are not sufficient to produce the existing reservoirs of oil.

Another interesting fact is that every oil field throughout the world has outgassing helium. Helium is so often present in large quantities that helium detectors are used as oil-prospecting tools. Helium is an inert gas known to be a fundamental product of the radiological decay of uranium and thorium, identified in quantity at great depths below the surface of the Earth, 200 and more miles below. The helium is not found in meaningful quantities in areas that are not producing methane, oil or natural gas. It is not a member of the dozen or so common elements associated with life. It is found throughout the solar system as a thoroughly inorganic product.

Gold was very clear about his view on petroleum and natural gas: 'Hydrocarbons are not biology reworked by geology but rather geology reworked by biology.'

Sir Fred Hoyle summed up the situation as he saw it, rather succinctly: 'The suggestion that petroleum might have arisen from some transformation of squashed fish or biological detritus is surely the silliest notion to have been entertained by substantial numbers of persons over an extended period of time.'

## Were Gold and Hoyle right about the world's oilfields being geologically formed?

There have been numerous reports in recent times of oil and gas fields not running out at the expected time, but instead showing a higher content of hydrocarbons after they had already produced more than the initially estimated amount. This has been seen across the planet from the Middle East to the deep gas wells of Oklahoma and in the Gulf of Mexico, as well as many other places. It is this apparent refilling during production that has been responsible for the gross underestimate of reserves that have been published time and again. In the early 1970s it was firmly predicted that by 1987 there would be a huge energy crisis as oil and gas wells ran dry, and that there would ensue a huge shift in the wealth of nations. The natural refilling of wells is an item of the greatest economic significance, and also a key to understanding what the source of all this petroleum had been.

Even more intriguing is evidence that several oil reservoirs around the globe are refilling themselves, such as the Eugene Island reservoir – not from the sides, as would be expected from parallel organic reservoirs, but from the bottom up. Dr Gold strongly believed that oil is a 'renewable, primordial soup continually manufactured by the Earth under ultrahot conditions and tremendous pressures. As this substance migrates toward the surface, it is attached by bacteria, making it appear to have an organic origin dating back to the dinosaurs.'

It was once thought that oil from the Middle East was a finite resource that could last 40 or 50 years at best. Yet over recent years, reserves have more than doubled. These fields have been methodically exploited since the first gusher was discovered. Today, OPEC is pumping around 30 million barrels of oil per day.

I was recently speaking to a director of a company involved with natural gas extraction, and asked if he was aware of the non-fossil origin explanation for gas and petroleum. The answer came back that he was well aware that these products are naturally occurring and not the product of fossilized remains. Yet science still teaches – as a given 'fact' rather than a popular but unproven theory – that petroleum is a fossil fuel, despite far greater logic to the contrary.

In August 2002 a paper by J F Kenney, V A Kutcherov, N A Bendeliani and V A Alekseev, about the genesis of hydrocarbons and the origin of petroleum, was published in *PNAS*. The authors argued that the hydrogen–carbon system does not spontaneously evolve hydrocarbons at pressures less than 30kbar, even in the most favourable environment. This system evolves hydrocarbons under pressures found in the mantle of the Earth and at temperatures consistent with that environment.

They stated later: '… competent physicists, chemists, chemical engineers and men knowledgeable of thermo-dynamics have known that natural petroleum does not evolve from biological materials since the last quarter of the 19th century.'

If experts like Gold, Kenney, Kutcherov, Bendeliani, Alekseev and Hoyle are correct, the big bogeyman scenario of 'the end of the petroleum age' simply will not happen. It is strange that free-thinking, world-class scientists and (at least some) oil industry practitioners think that oil is a geological component of the Earth's makeup rather than 'squashed fish'. Could it be that there are vested interests involved in this issue?

Oil-producing countries and oil-extraction companies both stand to gain financially by sticking with the fossil origin claim. If it is perceived to be a finite commodity prices will remain high, compared to a situation where it is accepted that there is an almost boundless supply bubbling up from inside our planet. In addition, governments like the fossil theory because it allows them to be seen as responsible in taxing an endangered fuel source.

Maybe the lack of interest in accepting that the Earth contains hydrocarbons, just like other star debris scattered around the cosmos, is no accident.

# Chapter 5

# OLD IDEAS DIE HARD

'It doesn't make any difference how smart you are, who made the guess, or what his name is. If it disagrees with experiment, it's wrong. That's all there is to it.'

*Richard Feynman*

Old ideas do not shift easily just because they are, or might be, wrong. A perfect example of wrong-headed group-think is the notion that, despite abundant evidence to the contrary, Christopher Columbus discovered America for Europeans. Back in 1996 my first book, *The Hiram Key*, was published, in which I discussed the case for pre-Columbian European visitors to the east coast of North America. The evidence put forward was intended to be thought-provoking because it could not, in itself, establish that Europeans had been on the continent prior to 1492. However, shortly after the book was published, new light was shed on the matter.

I was contacted by my literary agent to ask if I would take a phone call from Fred Olsen, the famous Norwegian shipping magnate and chairman of Fred. Olsen & Co. I was aware that he has a reputation for being a Scandinavian Howard Hughes due to his great wealth and preference for privacy, so I felt flattered that he wanted to speak to me. Besides running his business empire, Fred Olsen has a track record in investigative archaeology, having been closely involved with the exploits of explorer Thor Heyerdahl – including the famous *Kon-Tiki* voyage.

Mr Olsen rang the next day and spent around an hour and a half in conversation about my book in general and his knowledge of the history of transatlantic sailing. Fred began by stating that he wholeheartedly agreed that the notion that Christopher Columbus discovered America was foolish in the extreme. He stated that there probably has never been a time when Europeans were not travelling to the Americas.

Norwegians have always been great sailors, ever since their longboats attacked towns and villages around the northern European coast. I was fascinated to hear from Fred Olsen that the English west coast port of Bristol had been the most important staging post for Norwegian sailors for many centuries. He went on to say that there are extant maritime documents in that city that record frequent voyages to North America long before the time of Columbus.

Fred then surprised me greatly by stating that these sailors could cross the Atlantic from Bristol to what is now Canada without ever losing sight of land. He explained that they would make their way up the west coast of England and Scotland past the Hebrides and up to the islands of Orkney. From there they continued the 23 nautical miles from North Ronaldsay to the small island of Fair Isle, and on to Shetland less than 20 miles away. Then these late medieval vessels would turn towards the Faroe Islands, which are 150 miles distant. Once they reached the top of that group they had the long stretch to Iceland some 240 miles across the ocean, and from the north of that landmass it was another 150 miles of open water sailing to reach Greenland. The next leg is the 180 miles across to Baffin Island in North America, after which it is all plain sailing down the eastern coast as far as one wishes to travel.

The greatest distance across the open sea that had to be covered on this journey was the 240 nautical miles from the Faroes to Iceland. The mountain of Slættaratindur sits right at the north of the Faroe Islands, reaching 882m above sea level – and in the opposite direction Hvannadalshnúkur is the highest point on Iceland at 2,110m.

These distances are surprisingly small in terms of crossing the North Atlantic, but the span of 240 nautical miles seems a heck of a long way to cover without losing sight of land.

The formula for calculating the approximate horizon distance is 3.57 × the square root of the height of the observer or the distant object. Both mountains and the crow's nest on the ship's mast have values above sea level, which suggest that there would be a stretch of just over 70 (of the 240) miles when both mountains would be out of view, assuming good visibility.

However, as Fred Olsen was quick to point out, the atmosphere of the Earth changes this theoretical calculation quite considerably. Objects beyond the horizon appear in view long after they should have disappeared if there was no atmosphere on the planet. When you watch a sunset, for example, the Sun is actually completely below the horizon before it appears to even touch the sea.

This refraction of the line of sight means that the sailor in the crow's nest at the top of the mast would have made visual contact with the peak of Hvannadalshnúkur in southern Iceland just as he was losing sight of Slættaratindur on the northern side of the Faroe Islands.

Not only did Fred Olsen explain how these pre-Columbian transatlantic sailors made regular crossings of the ocean, he also claimed that the Roman Catholic Church had records of a bishopric in Newfoundland before Christopher Columbus was born. He even suggested that there was a case for believing that the Black Death, a form of plague, was taken to the New World by traders around the 1350s.

The Black Death had begun in the Gobi Desert around 1320 and it quickly spread across China, where it wiped out an estimated 35 million people. It was then transmitted across India and the Middle East to Europe. By 1350 the plague had killed a third of the entire Muslim world and was spreading throughout Europe. In Norway it killed more people than it spared and the infected sailors, it is claimed, took the disease to the native populations in North America.

Fred told me that he had good reason to believe that the population of cities in what is now the southern USA and Mexico were wiped out. This would explain why the Toltec people disappeared from history and their empty cities were later occupied by the Aztecs. The Aztecs recorded what they knew about the previous occupants and they adopted the Toltecs' history, including legends and spiritual mythologies, for themselves.

Is Fred Olsen right in claiming that people from Europe have 'always' sailed to the Americas – or is the standard Christopher Columbus discovery theory true? Recent discoveries suggest that Olsen is indeed correct about this matter.

The standard account of the human population in America is that mammal hunters entered the continent some 12,000 years ago via a land bridge that spanned the Bering Sea to form what is known as the Clovis culture. But new research from noted archaeologists Dennis J Stanford and Bruce A Bradley has put forward a new scenario. Applying rigorous scholarship, they have argued that the first Americans crossed the Atlantic by boat and arrived far earlier than previously thought. Supplying archaeological and oceanographic evidence to support this assertion, their book *Across Atlantic Ice: The origin of America's Clovis culture* dismantles the old paradigm whilst persuasively linking Clovis technology with the culture of the Solutrean people, who occupied France and Spain in the midst of the last Ice Age!

The case put forward by Stanford and Bradley is that, contrary to common belief, the first people to inhabit the Americas were not Asians walking across a land bridge spanning the Bering Sea, but people who sailed by boat from Europe between 25,000 and 13,000 years ago.

The point of this little story is to illustrate how it can be dangerous to take 'common knowledge' at face value. Whilst schools continue to teach children that Columbus 'discovered America' by landing on the Bahamas archipelago in 1492, the facts suggest something utterly different. The 'experts' are simply reciting the tribal myths of our civilization – rather than taking a scientific approach that results in new realities.

Unfortunately, this is an entirely normal situation, where new ideas are smothered by old conventions for the sake of preserving the reputations of ageing 'experts'.

## What's in a name?

There is a similar myth about the naming of the continent as 'America'. It is repeatedly claimed that the name came from Amerigo Vespucci, the famous Italian explorer, financier, navigator and cartographer. In fact, this attribution was a mistake by a young German priest and cartographer who called himself Martin Waldseemüller. In 1507 he was one of the first people to be involved in printing a book, which was called *Cosmographiae Introductio*. He recorded how the New World had been named after the Italian navigator. Only afterwards did he find that he had made a mistake, but once printed it was too late to stop the word from spreading. The name long predates Vespucci and possibly originated with the ancient name for Venus, which is the 'star' that the early navigators followed across the ocean to the west; it was known to the French Norse (Normans) as *la merica*.

The hard fact is that ships' records show that North America was frequently visited long before Columbus was even born. Whilst this belief that Columbus was the first European to land in America is a trivial example, it does illustrate how cultural beliefs can dominate, even when the real experts know better but sometimes choose not to tell the lay world.

# Chapter 6

# GOD IN THE MODERN WORLD

'I want to know how God created this world. I am
not interested in this or that phenomenon, in the
spectrum of this or that element. I want to know
His thoughts; the rest are details.'

*Albert Einstein*

Up until the beginning of the 20th century most people
belonged to an organized religion of some kind, and people
generally looked to their holy books to provide some meaning
to their lives – and their deaths. Today, particularly in the West,
there are huge numbers of people who no longer subscribe to
any faith system, although the majority appears still to believe
in some kind of God. A recent survey has shown that no fewer
than nine out of ten people across the world believe in God. Of
countries polled, Nigeria showed an astonishing 100 per cent
belief in God, and even the most doubting country of them all,
the United Kingdom, had two thirds of the people surveyed
reporting that they feel there must be some kind of higher power.

In February 2012 I carried out my own straw poll using a smartphone app, asking an unknown audience, 'Did God create the universe?' As I am a member of the Market Research Society in the UK, I realize that this little test is not exactly scientific, but it was revealing nonetheless. I broadcast the question and within minutes had well over 100 responses, mainly from the USA and the UK. The result was amazingly split down the middle with 51 per cent saying yes and 49 per cent saying no – but the British respondents were much more negative than their American counterparts.

The app allowed respondents to return comments if they wished, and some of these were interesting. One American said that 'God is the universe' – which seems a very reasonable idea. A female responded with certainty: 'Yes. If we evolved from apes then why are there still apes around now?' This is a classic example of false logic that causes many uncritical people to become believers and rational thinkers to be suspicious of all forms of religion.

There are more than 6 million practising Christians in the UK, and a further 29 million who consider themselves to be Christian in some loose sense. So, allowing for other, minority, faiths, over a quarter of the population believe in the existence of a higher power without having any interest in organized religion. God, it seems, is an innate concept for many people, even in the least religious society surveyed. In some societies, a belief in a higher power is not always associated with active participation in an organized religion. In Muslim countries, the sanctions against any exit from the dominant faith are severe, even if secularism has made progress in countries such as Egypt, Lebanon and Indonesia.

Israel, where as many as 80 per cent of Jewish citizens say they believe in God, is nonetheless a very secular society overall.

A belief in a higher power is hardly surprising. Each of us emerges suddenly into the vastness of space and time that we call the universe; we – it is hoped – then mature, slowly decline and finally prepare for our return to non-existence. To be given everything out of nothing and then lose it all again, just as we have really got to understand ourselves, is pretty tough. Also, it is rather scary to think that we are alone. All but the most independently minded people need someone to take responsibility for everything. Surely, the thinking goes, the 'buck' cannot stop with me – there has to be a 'parent' figure to help me and to take responsibility for my fallibilities?

And it is not only the fear of being alone in life; part of most religions promises that the return to nothingness can be avoided – but only if we stick to the rules of the priests concerned. And even if we do transgress, there is the suggestion that a bit of grovelling – or perhaps a payment to 'God's representative' – might sort things out. The 19th-century Iranian king, Nasir al-Din Shah, who had a very long beard and hundreds of wives and thousands of children, once paid good money to the eminent Arab cleric Shaykh Ahmad al-Ahsa'i. The cleric – a brilliant thinker, if a little on the heretical side – assured the king that there would be marriage in heaven, which seems to have taken a weight off his mind.

Of course, the word 'God' is remarkably flexible. You will find one definition at the beginning of this book, but for some it means the variously friendly or vengeful bearded father figure in heaven to whom one can pray, either in hope or out of fear. For others it describes nothing more than an abstract creative force that underpins the workings of the entire universe.

However, scientists today consider themselves to be more rational and sophisticated than past thinkers – even a truly great one like Isaac Newton. In the 20th century, science rapidly developed into an all-embracing and self-describing world-view that apparently explains the way things are. Intelligent people no longer need to believe in a God. In times past, the term 'superstition' described other people's misguided beliefs while the otherwise irrational beliefs of our own 'faith' were considered to be responsible spirituality. In the science-shaped world of the 21st century, the very thin line that divides superstition and religion has become questionable to some. Belief in anything that cannot be measured and recorded is, in some quarters, now considered foolish.

But believers do not give in easily. In the USA in particular there has been a resurgence of the Christian religion in new forms; forms that challenge the very basis of science. The rise of the Christian 'Creationists', for example, who argue that the universe only came into existence in the Late Stone Age – on Sunday 23 October 4004 BC, according to Archbishop Ussher – and that the theory of evolution is wrong because it contradicts their almost unbelievably unsophisticated simplistic interpretations of ancient Jewish texts. They have no sense of context for the texts and no sense of time frames, either astronomically, geologically or regarding human existence.

This 'crazy' end of the religious spectrum has caused some scientists to feel duty-bound to wage war against the very concept of God – any interpretation of what might be meant by God. British evolutionary biologist and popular science author Richard Dawkins has publicly denounced the principal tenets of Christianity, describing them as 'barking mad'. Although literal adherence to some of the more outlandish myths involved may, arguably, justify the use of those two words, is the idea of some underlying original purpose to the universe really a sign of insanity? Is a belief in the probability of a conscious cosmic grand plan any more ridiculous than some of the more speculative, supposedly scientific, ideas discussed in 'rational' circles?

It is probably fair to say that Dawkins is regarded as the most famous atheist in the world – but in a debate held at the University of Oxford in February 2012 he publicly admitted he could not be sure that God does not exist. He told the then Archbishop of Canterbury, Dr Rowan Williams, that he preferred to call himself an agnostic rather than an atheist. However, he stated that he had devised a seven-point scale, where one identifies a questioning believer and seven an atheist. He gave himself a score of 6.9, which presumably means that whilst he obviously cannot prove a negative, he considers God's existence to be unlikely in the extreme. Dawkins has explained his position by saying: 'I think the probability of a supernatural creator existing is very, very low... Today the theory of evolution is about as much open to doubt as the theory that the earth goes round the sun.'

Of course, it may well be that Dawkins is constructing a valid argument against the sort of personal, internalized God that is treated as a real person – someone who interacts with men, has a son with a young virgin, writes his memoirs, speaks out of a cloud, and so on – rather than a cosmic creative force that does none of these things and is easier to grasp by the rational, enlightened mind.

Dawkins' reference to the theory of evolution in this context shows that he considers it to be incompatible with the possibility of the existence of a creator. However, there are a huge number of people who totally accept the full-strength concept of evolution (from the single-cell amoeba through to Dawkins himself) and yet believe that God created the universe and everything in it.

Whilst religions are prone to produce stories of myth and magic, science has come up with its own set of apparently irrational concepts. Quantum physicists have produced a range of explanations for the way that the smallest pieces of the universe behave that does not sit comfortably with any normal sense of logic. Is it reasonable to believe that some physical objects have to rotate through 720 degrees to return to their original position? Is it rational to accept that some sub-atomic particles can communicate instantaneously with each other across the span of the entire universe? Both of these are acts of belief that fly in the face of the evidence of our eyes. However cogent the calculations and however well predictions are borne out by experiment, these beliefs appear to require more than a little 'faith'.

## Where science and belief meet

Are the concepts of empiricism and faith necessarily mutually exclusive? Apparently not, as far as most scientists are concerned, if the USA is typical.

According to a survey published in *Nature* in 1997, 40 per cent of scientists in the USA had a firm belief in God and a further 14.5 per cent described themselves as doubters or agnostics rather than outright rejecters. This indicates that only a minority of scientists are full-on atheists – a ratio that had not changed a jot over the preceding 80 years.

No doubt most laypeople are surprised to learn that so many scientists are open to the idea that there is a God. Take Colin Humphreys, a professor of materials science at the University of Cambridge, who believes that life on Earth evolved through the action of natural selection upon random mutation. But he also holds that it is an historical truth that Moses led his people out of Egypt and communicated with God on Mount Sinai. Humphreys has researched the subject in depth and says: 'I believe that the scientific world view can explain almost anything... But I just think there is another world view as well.'

Another example of a religious scientist is Russell Stannard, an emeritus professor of physics, who embraces the fantastic ability of science to describe the workings of matter, time and space. But he starts out with perhaps the most fundamental question of them all: 'Why is there something rather than nothing? Why is there a world?'

It has to be true that nothing is much more likely than us existing. Logic suggests that there was nothing before the Big Bang (if that theory is correct), but it is a false logic because there cannot have been 'nothing' before time existed.

It kind of follows that God could not have been around to decide to cause the eruption of time and space out of a single point of less than nothing. The argument is that the concept of time has no meaning before the beginning of the universe. This was first pointed out by St Augustine of Hippo in the 5th century. When asked: What did God do before he created the universe? Augustine replied to the effect that time was a property of the universe that God created, and that time did not exist before the beginning of the universe.

Some intellectuals, such as the late Professor Anthony Flew, built their reputations on a total rejection of the concept of God. As one of the most respected philosophers of his generation, Flew belonged to the analytic and evidentialist schools of thought, and he frequently focused on the philosophy of religion. He was a powerful advocate of atheism, arguing that one should presuppose atheism until empirical evidence of a God surfaces.

In his book *How to Think Straight*, Flew pointed out that practical reasoning and clear thinking are essential for everyone who wants to make proper sense of the information we receive each day. He stressed the importance of being able to know quickly the difference between valid and invalid arguments, the contradictory versus the contrary, vagueness and ambiguity, contradiction and self-contradiction, the truthful and the fallacious. These, he said, are the qualities that separate clear thinkers from the crowd.

After 66 years of acclaimed work this clear thinker and champion of atheism shocked the academic world by suddenly announcing that science appeared to have proven the existence of God. Flew's reason for his monumental volte-face was the discovery of evidence that indicated to him that some sort of intelligence must have created the world we inhabit. He pointed in particular to the investigation by biologists of DNA, which has shown that an unbelievable complexity of arrangements are needed to produce life –

leading to the unavoidable conclusion that intelligence must have been involved.

Flew first rocked the atheist community when he sent a letter to the August–September 2004 issue of the *Philosophy Now* journal, in which he stated: 'It has become inordinately difficult even to begin to think about constructing a naturalistic theory of the evolution of that first reproducing organism.'

When asked if his startlingly new ideas would upset some people, he replied: 'That's too bad… My whole life has been guided by the principle of Plato's Socrates: Follow the evidence, wherever it leads.'

Anthony Flew died in April 2010 believing that the universe had been designed and that there was therefore a 'God'. He did not, however, see any connection between that 'fact' and any concept of life after death – which he fully rejected. But even so, he must have died a happy man.

What would happen if hard, testable, science-based evidence for the reality of a creator God became available? Would scientists embrace God? Would science and religion become reunited once again?

The main issue that caused Anthony Flew finally to conclude that there must be a God was the existence of life – most particularly the improbability of DNA having come into existence by accident.

It is time to consider what we mean by life and to look closely at the role of DNA.

# Chapter 7

# THAT ODD STATE
# CALLED LIFE

'We have a lot of really, really strange coincidences,
and all of these coincidences are such that they
make life possible.'

*Andrei Linde*

The term 'life' gets used in a very broad way by most people.
People speak of extraterrestrial life, despite the fact that
none has ever been found, and expressions such as artificial
intelligence (AI) can be seen to blur the boundary between the
living and the non-living. Whilst life is easy to see around us,
it is actually very difficult to define. Everything that is organic?
When does a fertilized egg become a living entity? At what
point in the endgame is a creature actually dead?

Life can be defined as the condition that distinguishes
animals and plants from inorganic matter, including the
capacity for growth, reproduction, functional activity and
continual change preceding death. However, crystals come
very close to fitting the bill.

In February 2013 the highly respected journal *Science* published an article that demonstrated just how close crystals can be to life forms. 'Living Crystals of Light-Activated Colloidal Surfers' was written by a team from the Department of Physics, New York University (NYU), and the Department of Physics and Chemistry, Brandeis University, Waltham, Massachusetts.

They created what they called two-dimensional 'living crystals', which form, break, explode and re-form elsewhere. The dynamic assembly results from a competition between self-propulsion of particles and an attractive interaction induced respectively by osmotic and phoretic effects and activated by light. The self-organizing behaviour the scientists created used particles made of cubes of hematite, a compound made of iron and oxygen. Each particle is contained within a sphere-like polymer coating, with one corner left exposed. When hit with blue light, the cubes conduct electricity. When placed in a hydrogen peroxide bath in blue light, the exposed tips set off reactions. Random forces may pull the crystals apart, but they can merge again. The process repeats itself over and over. It stops when you turn off the light switch.

'Here we show that with a simple, synthetic active system, we can reproduce some features of living systems,' Jeremie Palacci of NYU said. 'I do not think this makes our systems alive, but it stresses the fact that the limit between the two is somewhat arbitrary.'

The formal listing of life includes all organisms from cyanobacteria to plants and animals, and the single most defining feature is the ability to reproduce: the formation of identical or almost identical copies of a complex structure from simple starting materials. This local increase of complexity (or decrease of entropy) appears to contradict the Second Law of Thermodynamics, which states that entropy must always increase in natural spontaneous processes. However, it can be argued that overall entropy always increases so long as the changes in the surroundings as well as the changes in the organisms themselves are considered. Viewed this way, there is no conflict between the basic laws of physics and chemistry and the existence of living organisms. But, as life forms are self-contained entities, the new sciences of biochemistry and molecular biology have had to be created with their own concepts, principles and laws in addition to those of physics and chemistry.

It would be easy to believe that there is a chasm between simple living entities, such as bacteria, and us humans at the top of the evolutionary tree. But things are not quite that simple. Your body obviously is made up of countless human cells containing your DNA, but you may be surprised to learn that those exclusively human bits of you are a small minority of your body mass. Around 60 per cent of our body weight is water – but of the living matter less than one tenth is actually human. The remaining 90 per cent of that living matter is made up of other life forms – billions of individual creatures with their own DNA living in a symbiotic relationship.

Despite it being your body, we are essentially outnumbered ten to one by other creatures.

These fellow passengers allow you to function as a mobile, conscious and reproductive unit. These non-human cells are mostly bacteria but also nematodes and other organisms, and this does not even take into account the huge numbers of viruses that are everywhere. The fact is, we are not single entities at all – every human being is a walking ecosystem!

Another strange fact is that one form of these alien entities has been with us since we were little more than microbes ourselves. Mitochondria are physically independent structures that contain their own DNA designated as mtDNA, which is inherited by humans down the female line. Analysis of mtDNA in the brain tissue of females has allowed very accurate mapping of evolutionary relationships, leading to the conclusion that modern humans evolved in Africa.

Another strange fact to come out of DNA research is that the extinct species of humans, which used to share the planet with us, have not left at all. The so-called Neanderthals, known for their brutish appearance, interbred with our ancestors remarkably recently and live on in our own genetic makeup. It has been determined that between 2 per cent and 4 per cent of the genetic blueprint of present-day non-Africans has come from Neanderthals. Anthropologist Erik Trinkhaus, of Washington University in St Louis, Missouri, who has long argued for Neanderthal–modern human interbreeding based on skeletal evidence, believes it could be far higher – maybe 10, or even 20, per cent.

Neanderthals are so closely related to modern man that some researchers group them and us as a single species. 'I would see them as a form of humans that are a bit more different than humans are today, but not much,' says Svante Pääbo, a palaeogeneticist at the Max Planck Institute in Leipzig, Germany, whose team recently sequenced the Neanderthal genome.

The common ancestor of humans and Neanderthals lived in Africa around half a million years ago. It is believed that the ancestors of Neanderthals moved north into Europe and Asia whilst our own ancestors remained in Africa until about 100,000 years ago, when they emerged and spread across the planet.

Recent research has found that Neanderthal DNA is not distributed uniformly across the human genome. Instead, it is more commonly found in parts of the coding that affect skin and hair. This apparently suggests that some gene variants provided a rapid way for modern humans to adapt to the new cooler environments they encountered as they moved north and east into what is now Europe and Asia. When the populations met, Neanderthals had already been adapting to these conditions for several hundred thousand years. 'It's tempting to think that Neanderthals were already adapted to the non-African environment and provided this genetic benefit to humans,' said Professor David Reich, from Harvard Medical School, co-author of a paper published in the journal *Nature*.

But other Neanderthal gene variants influenced modern human illnesses, such as type 2 diabetes, long-term depression, lupus, biliary cirrhosis (an autoimmune disease of the liver), Crohn's disease and – bizarrely – a liking for smoking.

However, although some of their DNA lives on in modern humans, the last Neanderthals died out in southern Europe around 25,000 years ago. The available evidence suggests that Neanderthals could talk, because they had the same language gene as modern humans. One cannot help but wonder what religious belief the Neanderthal people had. It would seem impossible for such an advanced species not to have done so.

## Bits of the Earth

Because we are Earthbound creatures at the top of the evolutionary chain, we tend to see ourselves as being separate from our planet but we are really just animated bits of the Earth itself. Any alien watching the Earth and seeing lumps of metal in the form of space probes being sent out would conclude that it was the Earth that was doing this. We humans are, in reality, just the thinking, mobile bits of the planet.

Given that humans are walking colonies of Earth-life, we have to also remember that all life on Earth is one. Everything works together – and humankind is the main beneficiary.

## Plants and drugs

Humans are at the top of what was once was called the 'food chain' but is now more frequently called the 'food web' because of the way that energy moves from species to species in a complex, rather than linear, way. Energy from the Sun is absorbed by plants, plants are eaten by herbivores, herbivores are eaten by carnivores and we humans eat them all. However, there are all kinds of exceptions, such as the Venus flytrap and the tropical pitcher plants of the genus *Nepenthes*, which can trap and consume small reptiles and mammals. And when we die we return to 'worm food' or at least release our carbon for use by other living creatures.

But plants have far more to do with our well-being than simply providing primary or secondary nutrition in the case of plant-fed livestock. How many people across the world every day suffer from a headache, and how many of those people reach for a bottle of aspirin, which has been known for many decades to assist in the relief of pain? Aspirin is now created chemically, in laboratories, but it was originally derived from the bark of the willow tree.

We know that from at least the 5th century BC people in different cultures were aware that a preparation made from the bark of certain willow trees could assist in pain relief, and it is probably reasonable to infer that this came about as a result of centuries of trial and error. After all, our ancient ancestors could not call at the pharmacy. All they had with which to treat themselves for any medical problem were the plants, minerals and animal-derived by-products in their immediate environment.

Herbal medicine, both Western and Asian, has re-emerged as an important adjunct to conventional methods since the 20th century, and in some cases it can be more effective than modern medicine for certain conditions. But it remains an object of mistrust for most conventional doctors.

In recent times, chemists isolated the chemical contained within the willow bark that helped to relieve pain. It is called salicin, and is now one member of a family of drugs known as salicylates, which have a range of pharmaceutical uses. Aspirin itself not only helps to relieve pain, but it also reduces blood clotting, to such an extent that this remarkable chemical may have contributed to saving the lives of numberless thousands of people with heart problems caused by obstructed blood vessels.

As a pain reliever aspirin, or more specifically salicin, works because it blocks prostaglandin, a substance created within the human brain and designed to register pain. Prostaglandin is vital. It tells us when we put our hand too close to a naked flame or when we are overstressing our muscles, but sometimes, in the case of a headache, it may be released due to stress or tension, and it is merely inconvenient. At such times we simply take an aspirin, or more likely these days one of the substitutes that science has learned to create.

Aspirin is far from being the most effective painkiller. There is an entire spectrum derived from nature, some of which can alleviate severe pain – such as morphine, an opium-derived drug extracted from that beautiful and fragile flower, the poppy.

One of the most potent painkillers of all is the Transcutaneous Electrical Nerve Stimulation (TENS) machine, a device that operates by blocking or modulating pain signals from the brain by using electrical stimulation delivered through thin wires and small pads. Although deemed very effective by its supporters, it remains controversial, perhaps because the makers of painkillers do not want competition.

Our brains have the ability to synthesize chemicals from the raw ingredients we intake naturally, which make us feel good, or even ecstatic. People who exercise regularly and hard often experience what is known as the 'runner's high', which is a feeling of well-being – sometimes to the point of euphoria. This is not simply the result of self-satisfaction with having done well but is caused because the brain releases chemicals called endorphins, enkephalins and dynorphins. What these chemicals do is to stimulate the production of another chemical called dopamine. It is dopamine that makes the athlete feel high and which covers up underlying pain as a result. Again, this natural process has a very important part to play in survival. An early hunter might have been injured whilst trying to cope with an aggressive prey species and in this situation the hunter could easily become the hunted. Dopamine production could allow the hunter to ignore his own injuries long enough to make a timely escape.

Endorphins and their companion chemicals were created by evolution and their existence within human beings has had a part to play in our survival, but what seems most remarkable is that the release of dopamine can be stimulated by something that has had nothing to do with human evolution – namely the residue of the sap from a poppy bud. In effect, opium and its derivatives have molecules of exactly the right shape to bind to the same receptors in the brain to which endorphins, enkephalins and dynorphins attach themselves.

We take such a fact for granted, but it is actually quite remarkable. The effects of a substance made from the opium poppy have been known since ancient times and once upon a time such happenings were considered to be within the remit of the gods. In ancient Greece the opium poppy was associated with the goddess Demeter, an earth goddess who was also associated with sleep and death. Opiates derived from the poppy were most likely used in Demeter's mystery rites and their medicinal qualities were known to numerous other ancient civilizations – and were usually attributed to divine intervention.

Why should a molecule derived from a plant – which, let's face it, is about as far from us in evolutionary terms as it is possible to be – just happen to do what it does to our brains? Clearly, in the case of the poppy, the production of

73

the milky fluid that contains opium serves some practical purpose as far as the plant is concerned, but the fact that it can and does have such a tremendous effect on human beings is almost entirely overlooked.

## Plant power

Long after the Prince of Wales invited derision by saying that plants respond to human speech, a recent study by the Royal Horticultural Society found that tomato plants do respond to the human voice; further investigations have shown that their communication skills are indeed much more advanced than previously thought.

Chemical messages exchanged between plants allow them to send out alerts when danger is present, such as an attack of pests or the presence of pollinators such as bees. In tests, sagebrush shrubs had their leaves 'clipped' as if they were being eaten by herbivores. Other sagebrush plants growing near the clipped shrubs proved more resilient than control plants without damaged neighbours, indicating that they had received warning of the threat.

'Plants not only respond to reliable cues in their environments but also produce cues that communicate with other plants and with other organisms,' said Richard Karban of the University of California, co-author of the study with Kaori Shiojiri of Kyoto University. The research, published in the journal *Ecology Letters*, showed that plants are 'capable of more sophisticated behaviour than we imagined', Professor Karban added.

## Plants and the brain

Further down the evolutionary tree than plants are relatively simple organisms known as fungi, which are considered to be a separate kingdom from plants, animals and bacteria. As well as the familiar mushrooms, fungi include useful entities such as the yeast species *Saccharomyces cerevisiae,* which has been used in baking and, more intriguingly, in fermenting alcoholic beverages, such as beer, for at least 9,000 years. Ethyl, otherwise known as ethanol alcohol, is the world's most popular drug. It acts on nerve cells deep in the brain, acting initially as a stimulant before inducing feelings of relaxation and mild euphoria. Like many preparations made by fungi and plants, alcohol in its various forms is believed to have positive effects on our well-being when taken in appropriate quantities. But when consumed in excess, considerable short-term and long-term damage can occur both physically and psychologically.

Recreational drugs have been used by humans for a very long time indeed. In 1976 nicotine was discovered in the mummified remains of Pharaoh Ramses II after it was brought to the Museum of Mankind in Paris. Then, in the early 1990s, the Egyptian Museum in Munich initiated a research project to find out whether the ancient Egyptians had consumed the lotus flower because of its psychedelic properties, a theory triggered by the many decorative lotus flowers in their temples. Dr Svetla Balabanova, a renowned toxicologist of the Forensic Medicine Institute in Ulm, examined nine mummies and found not lotus flower remains but an abundance of cocaine as well as nicotine. Such drugs come from the coca and tobacco plants, which existed only in the Americas and were supposedly unknown before Columbus allegedly discovered America.

To check her findings, Balabanova requested that three other laboratories repeat the test. All came up with exactly the same results. Even though these techniques are used in criminal lawsuits the world over and are considered 100 per cent accurate, the scientific world reacted furiously and denied the outcomes because it implies that there was contact between Egypt and the Americas thousands of years ago, which is regarded as absolutely impossible.

Psychedelic or hallucinogenic drugs extracted from plants, and sometimes reptiles, have been used the world over by shamans, who always seem to consider their purpose to be a means to open communications with the spirit world. Substances such as LSD polarized public opinion in the 1960s when Dr Tim Leary, an influential American psychologist, encouraged the use of LSD for its therapeutic, emotional and spiritual benefits and coined the saying 'Turn on, tune in, drop out'.

More recently, clinical research has been conducted by psychiatrist Dr Rick Strassman into the effects of mind-altering drugs, specifically dimethyltryptamine, known as DMT, a plant-derived substance, which is also produced naturally by the pineal gland that sits at the centre of the base of the brain. Strassman's findings are controversial but have been remarkably well received by many people. He identifies that the pineal gland naturally excretes DMT under certain specific conditions, such as religious ecstasy or exposure to large magnetic fields around massive rock formations. It is also triggered by drinking the South American brew known as *ayahuasca*, which contains DMT extracted from the shrub *Psychotria viridis,* a member of the coffee family.

Strassman took many years to gain the necessary authority to conduct controlled experiments with hallucination-inducing drugs on healthy volunteers. Once he was able to carry out his research at the University of New Mexico's School of Medicine, his 60 subjects reported bizarre meetings with unseen entities that had many common features. This led Professor Strassman to conclude that the pineal gland was a kind of receiver that had the ability to link the brain with levels of reality beyond the scope of our normal five senses.

The pineal gland is a very strange organ as it sits right inside the brain and yet is not part of it. Its excretion of DMT certainly has a major impact on some individuals. This has led to DMT being dubbed 'The Spirit Molecule', but many scientists are sceptical of Strassman's conclusions and will remain so until his work has been repeated by other suitably qualified people.

We humans really are just part of the living Earth. We do not live on our planet – we are the planet. Along with all of our fellow life forms we represent what might be a glorious experiment in creating high intelligence with every bit of Earth's life-force working towards its own development in general and human development in particular.

## Our close cousins – the mammals

Our relationship with other animals has always been a mixture of love and hate. Dogs have been our closest friends ever since we bred them from wolves sometime after the end of the last Ice Age. On the other hand we seek to kill animals that take our food or pass on diseases. For this reason rats and flies have always been considered fair game.

Whilst history has shown that we humans can have a very low regard for other people outside our tribe or social group, humans are apparently becoming increasingly 'humane'. Steven Pinker, the Canadian experimental psychologist, cognitive scientist and linguist, was prompted to observe that violence between people was dramatically less than in the past. He explained how his research came about: 'I was struck by a graph I saw of homicide rates in British towns and cities going back to the 14th century. The rates had plummeted by between 30 and 100-fold. That stuck with me, because you tend to have an image of medieval times with happy peasants coexisting in close-knit communities, whereas we think of the present as filled with school shootings and mugging and terrorist attacks. Then in Lawrence Keeley's 1996 book *War Before Civilization* I read that modern states at their worst, such as Germany in the 20th century or France in the 19th century, had rates of death in warfare that were dwarfed by those of hunter-gatherer and hunter-horticultural societies. That too, is of profound significance in terms of our understanding of the costs and benefits of civilization.'

There is a wealth of information available concerning our symbiotic relationship with higher animals and about the astonishing abilities that some animals possess – some discussed here earlier. One story reported in February 2014 was both interesting and moving. The account appeared on the front page of the *San Francisco Chronicle*, telling how a female humpback whale had become entangled in a web of crab traps and lines. The hundreds of pounds in weight caused her to struggle to stay afloat. The whale also had hundreds of yards of rope wrapped around her body, her tail, her torso and a line tugging in her mouth.

A fisherman spotted the whale just east of the Farallon Islands near San Francisco and he radioed for help. Within a few hours, a rescue team arrived. They determined that the whale was in real trouble and that the only way to save her was to dive in scuba gear and untangle her. The team worked for hours, carefully slashing through the labyrinth of lines with curved knives and eventually she was freed of all encumbrances.

The divers say that once the female humpback was free to move, she swam in what seemed like joyous circles. The whale then came back to each diver – one at a time – and gave each a nudge, pushing her rescuers gently around as if she was thanking them. Some divers said it was the most beautiful experience of their lives. The diver who cut the rope out of the whale's mouth said her eyes were following him the whole time. And he will never be the same.

# Chapter 8

# BELIEFS AND RELIGION

'The essence of all religions is one. Only their
approaches are different.'

*Mahatma Gandhi*

The idea of a single, cohesive creative force for the world and
everything in it is almost certainly very ancient indeed. Gods
probably came into the lives of people hundreds of thousands
of years ago, most likely based on sex, birth, hunting, climate,
crops, the sky and, of course, death.

Only with the advent of writing can we really understand
the details of religious beliefs of early civilizations, such as
those of Sumer (Mesopotamia) and ancient Egypt. These
civilizations worshipped a pantheon of gods and goddesses,
deities which often fused and evolved as time went on. But
it seems that even within these early polytheistic religions
people had a need for a progenitor god or goddess responsible
for creation itself. It seems probable that theology became
more fragmented over the years, with more and more aspects
of life becoming associated with their own deity. Some forms

of monotheism reintroduce the polytheism of the past by assigning fresh roles and names to old gods, as in the Christian use of thousands of saints to carry out specific functions, to protect certain categories of person, even to serve as patrons of entire communities or nations. Although Islam has been the strictest of monotheisms after Judaism, its history is peppered by holy men, mainly Sufi saints whose shrines are the object of pilgrimages just like those in Christianity or Judaism. Jewish lore emphasizes the role of the righteous figure known as a *tzadik*, and North Africa in particular is home to many Jewish shrines, which are often visited by Muslims. Even a non-theistic religion like Buddhism still preserves the divine in the person of numerous saints, many known as *bodhisattva*s, such as Bodhidharma, the founder of Zen Buddhism. Tibetan Buddhism retains a pantheon of gods and saints, many linked to magical powers and a strong emphasis on mortality and the next world. In the short-lived but significant Babi religion of Iran (1844–1860s), it was not uncommon to refer to certain individuals as returning sacred figures in Islamic history.

As the last Ice Age ended, the climate warmed, mammoths disappeared and animals such as reindeer and horses started to move northwards. Slowly forests spread, red deer, wild pigs and cattle began to prosper. Dogs were the first animals to be domesticated; they were followed later by goats, sheep, cattle and pigs, which all existed in domesticated varieties by 6000 BC.

It seems that women led the way in the cultivation of plants, and they probably invented potting, spinning and weaving whilst their men took care of the herds and used oxen to pull ploughs. The first houses were simple round structures, but soon multiple groups of buildings sharing resources formed into villages.

One of the oldest cities in the world to be continuously occupied is Jericho, which had at least 2,000 people ten millennia ago – that is a full 6,000 years before Joshua of Old Testament fame arrived to allegedly bring down the stone-built city wall. Between 6250 and 5400 BC the city of Catal Huyuk in what is now Turkey had a large population and a religion centred on bulls. The many bull skulls and horns found in the homes of these people indicate that some kind of religious rituals were conducted, and the human bones of their forebears were buried below the floor in their houses.

By the time that history began – defined by the invention of writing – the world of humans was teeming with deities.

However, the distinction between the modern Western preference for monotheism and the 'old' idea of polytheism is largely imaginary. Those, such as Hindus, who still identify a web of integrated gods, are only teasing out elements of a great single entity. And those who demand belief in a great single God describe so many subsets that it is meaningless to make a distinction between the one and the many. In Christianity, for example, is 'God the Father' different from the 'Son' or the 'Holy Ghost', or are they a single entity? Surely the concept of the 'Holy Trinity' (where they are simultaneously three and one) is illogical and meaningless? And the Virgin Mary is treated almost as another deity – as are all the saints and angels that populate the kingdom of heaven.

Some 6,000 years ago the Sumerian civilization that occupied the land around the Tigris and Euphrates rivers began to narrow the act of creation down to three specific deities: Anu, god of the sky; Enlil, god of the air; and Enki, god of water. Later, the Babylonians adopted many of the early Sumerian creation myths and built on them, putting together a scenario that ultimately found its way into Judaism, which in turn led to the single 'father deity' with which much of the world is now so familiar. The memory of these early deities still exists in the Old Testament; after Abraham left his home city of Ur in Sumer to travel to Egypt he refers to 'the God of our Fathers' – meaning his family's ancestral deity.

The ancient Egyptians identified a progenitor god but also worshipped a vast conglomeration of other gods and goddesses who were tied to every facet of human life in the Nile Valley. The Egyptians were in no doubt that the first god was named Atum. In the beginning he existed in a watery void, which was called Nu; Nu in due course became the deification of this primordial abyss, as an androgynous deity with male and female aspects. Atum first created a hill upon which he could stand and in this tradition the hill eventually became the temple of Heliopolis. Because Atum was alone, he first mated with his own shadow – though it has to be said that the term 'he' may be inappropriate because Atum was known as the 'he–she' god and so did not really possess a single gender. Other gods followed from this union, but they became lost in the primeval waters. Atum wept at the loss of his children and his tears fell to the ground, where they became people.

Another Egyptian creation myth tells the story of Khepri, a scarab form of the sun god Ra. (The scarab beetle was held in awe by early Egyptians. The young of the scarab emerged from balls of dung and to observers it looked as though they had arisen from nothing – which, of course, only gods could do. The scarab had actually laid its eggs in the dung.) Khepri, many Egyptians believed, created plants and animals, but even in this version of the story it was the tears of Atum that became men and women.

In the Indian subcontinent another of the world's early major civilizations developed with the Indus Valley civilization, which began around 3300 BC. Also known as the Harrapan civilization, it covered a vast area in what is now Pakistan, Afghanistan and northern India, and originated much of what later developed into Hinduism, the world's oldest surviving religion. Hinduism does have a progenitor god, Vishnu, who, one myth suggests, lay sleeping within the coils of a giant snake. Vishnu and his guardian serpent slept silently in a huge ocean, but they were disturbed by a gentle humming, which grew in intensity until Vishnu awoke. Eventually, from Vishnu's navel a beautiful lotus flower grew and at its centre was the god Brahma. Vishnu told Brahma that the time had come to create the world and Brahma carried out his Lord's will.

Further east, in China, creation stories also developed very early. In one of these the first god, Pangu, was trapped within a vast black egg that also contained both Heaven and Earth combined. Pangu cleaved his way out of the egg with a great axe and the egg separated into Earth and Heaven. Although Pangu was clearly a god, he eventually died, and when he did his beard and hair became the night's stars, his skin took on the form of flowers and trees, his breath was the wind, his voice was thunder and his eyes became the Sun and the Moon.

Elsewhere in the world, some groups believed that creation took place at the behest of animals, whilst to others the whole business was entirely spontaneous. However, in the majority of creation myths a number of characters ultimately took part in what would eventually become the world we know and creation was separated into gods and people.

Although it might be said that the notion of one, single deity first developed in Egypt during the reign of Akhenaten c1330 BC, who introduced the single, all-powerful Aten, the failure of Akhenaten's project and the erasure of his name throughout Egypt mean that his monotheism lapsed and was largely forgotten. It was from the beliefs of a nation of (at first) loosely allied pastoralists in the Near East that our Abrahamic conception of God developed. These people, the Hebrews, are thought to have settled in Canaan some time during the second half of the second millennium BC. As nomads they had worshipped a formidable storm god found in the mountainous region of the Sinai Peninsula. This god was described in the Old Testament as a petulant and aggressive entity who, when annoyed by people, would kill them by firing a bolt of energy from inside the wooden box called the Ark. He also ordered the Hebrews to massacre the entire populations of cities. It was this deity, combined with elements of Sumerian/Babylonian tradition, that eventually coalesced into the single entity called Yahweh – the God of the Jews, and later of Christianity and Islam.

These three belief systems are the most powerful religions in the world today, with an estimated 2.2 billion Christians and around 1.6 billion Muslims, although there are perhaps only 14 million Jews. Other religions include 1 billion Hindus, 500 million Buddhists and 500 million followers of Chinese Folk Religions.

As to humanity's relationship with this one great creator, attitudes differ from religion to religion and even from sect to sect within the religions. However, all agree that in the beginning there was nothing 'but' God and that it was God who took the decision to create the universe and, within it, humans. It is suggested that this one, all-powerful God maintains a special relationship with humanity, which is seen as the pinnacle of his creation and which has a special part to play in his plans. It is even suggested that mankind was given dominion over all other animals and plants, and that humans are closer to God than any other creature.

Within early Judaism, Yahweh was frightening and bad tempered, but through modern Judaism, Islam and Christianity humanity developed a closer and more personal relationship with God, who can be directly approached through prayer and asked to intercede in the affairs of people. This is achieved to an even greater extent in Christianity through the intercession of Jesus Christ, who it is suggested was a human form of God (and God's Son) who lived and died as any other human being does, but who returned to life before ascending to heaven to be 'as one' with God.

Islam developed later than Christianity, having come into existence in AD 610 when Muhammad, a prophet, first dictated the verses of the Quran. This holy book was 'revealed' to Muhammad over a period of 22 years by the Archangel Gabriel, one of the numerous names and concepts he borrowed from Jews in the region. In its first few centuries, Islam spawned many great thinkers, astronomers, chemists, mathematicians and socially aware leaders – something it has not done for several hundred years – but it continued to follow its original social concept, whereas Christianity developed in a different way that ultimately gave birth to the modern, developed world and to science. By the Middle Ages, a doctrine had taken firm hold of Islam stating that *al-bid'a kufr* ('innovation is heresy') – a belief that placed ultimate power of life and death in the hands of Muslim religious leaders, since the penalty for apostasy in Islam is death.

Islam, like Judaism, is traditionally strongly opposed to any form of intercession and rejects Christian beliefs in the Trinity and Jesus being the Son of God. Nevertheless, both Shi'ism and Sufism – as well as the Ishraqi philosophy of Safavid Shi'ism and the complex philosophy of Shaykh Ahmad ibn Zayn al-Din al-Ahsa'i – have fostered a range of practices (rituals, pilgrimage and chanting in circles) that heighten the devotional response of celebrants and bring them into dynamic contact with *shaykh*s, *pir*s, *imam*s and all the other saintly figures, living and dead, who serve as intermediaries with the divine world.

Baha'ism is a religion that emerged from some heretical forms of Shi'ism in the 19th and 20th centuries and has now spread to almost every country in the world. At its heart is the belief that God reveals himself to man at long intervals, sending a human being (Moses, Buddha, Jesus and Muhammad) who is also a 'Manifestation of God' (*mazhar-e elahi*). This is a strong form of intercession. In his own writings, the founder, Baha' Allah, advances claims to be God incarnate.

Judaism is built strongly around the singularity of God. The Shema, an affirmation of Judaism and a declaration of faith in one God, is required to be recited each morning and night by all faithful Jews. The first line – 'Hear O Israel, the Lord is our God, the Lord is One' (*Shema Yisrael Adonai eloheinu Adonai Ehad*) – defines their belief in a single God. In very early Judaism, such as during the reigns of Solomon and David, many gods were given great respect. Indeed, the word *eloheinu* means 'our God', to distinguish Him from other gods (*elohim*). Nevertheless, some forms have developed in the past few centuries, notably Hassidic and Haredi Judaism, in which intercessory forms are employed. Some German and Polish prayerbooks (from about the 18th century) contain prayers that call on angels to intercede for the believers before God.

Christianity remained all-powerful to its adherents for many centuries, but there were many forms of the religion, the most powerful of which, the Roman Catholic Church, was centred in western Europe and based in Rome. The Catholic Church once had an iron grip but this power has slowly eroded from the Renaissance onwards and religion has very gradually had to share its social authority with secular bodies as rationalism developed in western Europe.

Freed from the total authority of the Church, and especially from the ability of the priests to put to death anyone who disagreed with its doctrines, scholars began to look elsewhere for models upon which to base their beliefs. Most of these early models came from ancient Greece, where philosophers had been at liberty to contemplate the world in a rational sense. People such as Archimedes, Aristotle, Plato, Pythagoras and Socrates had been able to look at the world freed from the constraints of religious belief. They sought to understand the natural, underlying principles upon which the world was based and their work became central to the rise of rationalism in western Europe.

In the knowledge explosion that the Renaissance spawned, people who became highly educated began to question the authority of the Church and some even considered whether or not everything that took place in a 'natural' world needed to be attributed to a supernatural deity. Early scientists began to look at astronomy in particular and to attribute quite natural laws to the movement of the planets, placing the Sun at the centre of the solar system for the first time. In several places, a quasi-religious philosophical tradition emerged. Alchemy employed mystical, religious and magical concepts in vain attempts to create the Philosopher's Stone, to turn base metal into gold and silver, and to find an elixir that would confer everlasting life. Even if these goals were never realized, alchemy did pave the way for what became chemistry from around the 18th century.

Chemists, anxious to further processes that would help industry to develop began to learn about the very components of life, which they discovered could be understood and manipulated. Something of a revolt against the constraining hand of religion began to develop in societies, to the point that many new, independent forms of Christianity emerged – such as the Dutch Reformed Church, Pietism in Germany and Methodism in England. Other people became agnostic.

This flow of reasoned thinking eventually led to a mechanistic view of human existence that apparently contradicted the explanation provided in ancient scriptures. In the mid-Victorian period, British naturalist Charles Darwin was able to show a plausible route by which humanity had been able to take its predominant place in the world – a route that in Darwin's estimation did not necessarily require an all-powerful deity. This was the process of natural selection, whereby 'happy accident' led to incremental improvements in species as those better suited to their environment survived and reproduced whereas the less successful died out.

Darwin had attended a Church of England school and then the University of Cambridge with the sole aim of becoming a clergyman. However, he developed a great interest in natural history, and science in general, and came to view organized religion as little more than a 'tribal survival strategy'. Yet Darwin always maintained his belief in God as the ultimate lawgiver and the First Cause.

However, real science (as opposed to academic convention) is far subtler than a case of just the 'good guys' versus the 'baddies'. There are few absolute truths in science, and whilst Darwin's observations were unquestionably brilliant, they are not to be taken too far.

Those who believe in evolution as nothing more than a happy accident in the organization of matter should perhaps ask themselves why evolution (natural selection) should exist at all. Why isn't the universe just a great morass of swirling chaos without order of any kind? Where does the propensity towards organization and increased complexity come from? This question is the meeting point of the scientific and the theological, where the two subjects look like sides of the same coin.

The theory of evolution is still regarded as one of the greatest intellectual revolutions, probably equal in importance to the theory of heliocentrism put forward in the 3rd century BC by Aristarchus of Samos, which states that the Earth revolves around the Sun.

Although Darwin may be spot on with his observations and broad conclusions, in what way do they detract from the probability of there being a God? Back in the 19th century when Darwin first shared his new ideas with the world, they did not go down too well with everyone, unsurprisingly.

Certain sections of the Christian establishment ridiculed the idea – 'obviously crazy' – that people had descended from monkeys rather than having been created instantly and wholly formed by God. Yet within his own lifetime Darwin's theory became accepted by almost all scientists and even many leading churchmen.

Things had taken rather longer for Aristarchus, as his Sun-centric idea was ignored by other astronomers at the time, and it was another 1,800 years before a fully predictive mathematical model of a heliocentric system was produced by a canon called Nicolaus Copernicus, who also happened to be a brilliant mathematician and astronomer. In the 17th century, the heliocentric model was expanded by Johannes Kepler and supporting observations were made by astronomer Galileo Galilei, using his telescope. By the 1920s Edwin Hubble had shown that our solar system was just a small part of the Milky Way galaxy among billions of other galaxies across an infinite universe.

In many ways the two ideas, of the solar system and evolution, are at the heart of what God stands for – at least as far as believers are concerned. The origins of mankind and the nature of heaven and Earth are fundamental to all religions.

# Chapter 9

# A PROTECTED PLANET

'You carry Mother Earth within you. She is not outside
of you. Mother Earth is not just your environment.'
*Thich Nhat Hanh*

Sometime around 4.6 billion years ago a new star was born. As
a result of interactions we do not yet fully understand, particles
of dust and gas started to coalesce into an area of increasing
density.

The greater the mass of an object, the greater its gravitational
pull, so, as the particles grew in number, companion particles
were drawn into what was a rapidly spinning proto-star. As the
density of the object became ever greater it began to spin faster
and faster, and eventually took on the form of a sphere. Thanks
to the wonderful laws of physics, the denser the core of the
body got, the hotter it became – until eventually it became
so dense and hot that hydrogen atoms were fused together
and began to produce helium, at the same time sending forth
massive bursts of energy into the surrounding space. As the
body grew more and more massive so did its gravity and it

gradually drew in all the surrounding material, which added to its overall size. Eventually, it stood alone in its own region of space, apart from a flattened field of debris that orbited it – the remnants of its own creation. A new star had been born and this was the star that we call the Sun.

All the gas and fine particles in the region that had not been drawn into the Sun itself eventually formed a series of rings, running around the equator of the Sun, a little like the rings of Saturn that we can still see today. With the passing of millions of years these fine particles began to collide and to gain a mass that, through gravitation, drew other particles and more gas together. As more time passed, so these bodies became larger, attracted still more debris and eventually formed the planets of the solar system.

Nearest to the Sun is Mercury, then Venus, Earth, Mars, Jupiter, Saturn, Uranus and Neptune. The status of tiny Pluto – just a fifth the mass of the Earth's Moon – as a planet or planetoid has changed back and forth over the years.

Mercury, Venus and Mars are Earth-like planets, in that they are relatively small and composed mainly of rock, whereas all the planets from Jupiter out are large and gaseous, and with many times the mass of any of the terrestrial-type planets. Between Mars and Jupiter is a region of asteroids, which are thought either once to have composed another terrestrial-type planet that was torn apart by Jupiter's massive gravitational field or to have never been able to come together as a planet because of it.

Of all the matter that coalesced into spheroid lumps those billions of years ago, only one has produced life: the planet Earth.

# A haven for life

Life requires many special circumstances that begin with the most basic rules of matter. As already discussed, the improbable laws of physics conspire in the most improbable manner to permit life.

At our own, more local, level the miracle of life on Earth is due to a concentration of many other equally critical factors – starting with the incredibly narrow temperature band that provides us with liquid water.

Water is, quite simply, the most wonderful and bizarre substance in the entire universe. All of life is utterly dependent on this molecule made up of one oxygen and two hydrogen atoms connected by covalent bonds. The mineral-rich oceans of the Earth freeze at around −1.91°C and boil at 102.7°C, whilst the boiling point of pure water occurs at 100°C at sea level.

The Earth is a beautifully balanced place. The coldest temperature ever recorded was −89.2°C (−128.6°F) at the Vostok Station in Antarctica and the highest was 58°C (136°F) at El Azizia in Libya. That is a range of absolute extremes of less than 148°C, which is utterly minuscule in terms of the possible range. The coldest anything can get is known as 'absolute zero', when atomic and molecular motion becomes almost stationary. This occurs at a rather chilly −273.15°C (−459.67°F). On the other hand there is no known upper limit for temperature, but the hottest spot in our solar system is the Sun's core, which comes in at an impressive 15,000,000°C.

The Earth is the only place we are aware of in the entire universe that could produce and sustain intelligent life forms in any way we can comprehend. A tour of our own solar system would surely make you wish you had stayed at home!

Your first stop would probably be the Moon, which happens to contain the coldest location in our solar system, despite its relative closeness to the Sun. Readings taken by NASA's Lunar Reconnaissance Orbiter revealed that temperatures near the Moon's south pole are a knee-knocking −240°C, a mere 33°C shy of absolute zero.

The title of the wettest place on Earth is claimed by a village named Mawsynram in the East Khasi Hills district of Meghalaya state, in northeastern India. It experiences an average annual rainfall of an astounding 11,872mm (almost 40ft). According to the *Guinness Book of World Records*, Mawsynram received an almost unbelievable 26m (more than 83ft or near to 14 fathoms) of rain in 1985. To put this into perspective, it would take Washington DC more than a quarter of a century to accumulate this volume of rainfall!

However, this wettest of wet spots on our home planet pales into insignificance when compared to Saturn's largest moon, Titan, where you would observe solid rocks of water ice drenched in near-constant, black, ethane rain at −180°C.* This super-cold rain produces giant hydrocarbon (gasoline) lakes and seas fed by networks of methane rivers. The methane then evaporates slowly to form clouds to complete the cycle with further downpours of what is essentially rocket-fuel rain. Despite these nightmare conditions on

---

* At Titan's super-cold temperature (−180°C/−292°F), $H_2O$ is a rock; it is not a volatile, not a fluid and not an ice, in the sense that you think of ice as a malleable solidified form of a fluid – it is a rock as hard as granite and it acts like granite.

Titan, it remains one of the few places in the solar system where experts believe life, in some form or other, just might have begun.

Our nearest neighbour is the red planet Mars, which has an atmosphere consisting almost entirely of carbon dioxide with just 0.2 per cent oxygen. The average pressure at the surface is about 0.6 per cent of that on Earth, yet the surface is bedevilled by frequent storms that last for many days. And more occasionally there are mega-storms of very fine dust particles, some 50 times larger than anything ever seen on Earth, which rip across the planet's entire surface.

Our neighbour on the other side is Venus, the hottest planet in the solar system. Here the surface temperature is a uniform 462°C and the surface pressure of its carbon dioxide atmosphere is 96 times greater than that on Earth – creating a crushing surface pressure equivalent to being at a depth of nearly one kilometre beneath the Earth's oceans. The Venusian atmosphere consists almost wholly of sulphuric acid. Space probes sent to Venus measure their survival rates in terms of minutes once they enter this super-hot, high-pressure, acid world.

Overall, other than our Earth, the solar system is not a life-friendly place.

Things do not appear to improve for advanced life beyond our solar system. In June 2010 astronomers using a powerful telescope in Chile were observing a planet orbiting a Sun-like star 150 light years (nearly 1.5 million, billion kilometres) away in the constellation of Pegasus. Despite this enormous distance and the fact that the planet is only 60 per cent the size of Jupiter, they were able to estimate the speed of winds ripping across its surface. They found that these winds were blowing at a truly astonishing 10,000kmph (6,250mph) – that is, more than eight times the speed of sound on Earth.

Earth, then, is very special. The normal temperature range on our home planet's surface is such that there are very few parts of the landmass that cannot readily support human life. We have a normal range of body temperature of 36.1–37.8°C (97–100°F), and yet the Inuit people live happily within the Arctic Circle and groups such as the Bedouin of Saudi Arabia and Aboriginal Australians prosper under baking desert heat.

The world's average temperature fluctuates slightly around the 14.5°C (58°F) mark, which is comfortable for physical work. Of course, it is entirely logical to conclude that we humans have evolved in the way we have because our environment is this temperature – but this is not a complete explanation. We could just as well have evolved in a world where only small sections of the planet were available to us to inhabit. No other known planet has a narrow temperature band that permits most of the water to be liquid most of the time.

More than two thirds of the Earth's surface is covered by water. The oceans hold 97 per cent of all the water on the Earth, and although less than 1 per cent is available as fresh surface water we have so much of this liquid that we survive quite easily. The ocean provides us with a source of food, energy and minerals, but above all else the sea helps keep the planet's climate healthy by regulating air temperature and by supplying moisture to produce rainfall. If there were no oceans, life would not exist on our planet. On Earth we can see water at the same time in its three states – as a solid in the form of ice, as a liquid in the form of water and as a gas in the form of clouds. Each water molecule is composed of just two atoms of hydrogen and one of oxygen and yet it acts as a universal solvent with a high surface tension.

Perhaps most surprising of all is how its density changes. Water has its maximum density at 4°C, which means that it not only gets lighter as it warms from that point, it also gets lighter as it cools. As everyone knows, warm water rises as convection currents, but it is also true that ice floats. Other planets and moons in our solar system may have some ice or steam but only the Earth is awash with life-bringing liquid water.

Liquid water has been absolutely crucial in creating the world we know today and, as far as is known, life itself cannot exist without it. As surely as plate tectonics and the Earth's hot core constantly create new mountain ranges, via volcanoes and the pushing up of mountains as landmasses meet, so water is mainly responsible for flattening them again. Constant weathering crumbles away the rocks as mountains age and water in the form of rain, ice and snow is primarily responsible. Liquid water, as streams and rivers, also disperses the weathered rock, carrying it down to the plains where it is distributed across flatter land, bringing much-needed nutrients to nourish life. Even more nutrients are carried by the rivers to the oceans, where they offer the necessary food for aquatic plants that stand at the bottom of the oceanic food chain.

If the overall temperature of the Earth changed even slightly or there was an alteration in the seasonal patterns, the nature of the water on our planet would change. The temperature of the Earth is one factor, another is the speed of the planet's rotation on its axis. Whilst all astronomical objects spin in some direction (Uranus spins on its side relative to the Sun), the rate varies greatly. Our own Moon, for example, rotates once for every 27.322 days of the Earth's orbit.

If Earth's spin slowed down, our days would become progressively longer, and if it slowed considerably the oceans would migrate north and south, leaving a single continent running around the entire equator. The air would also move north, making living on the great equatorial continent all but impossible. It is unlikely that humans would have emerged under such conditions – and we would probably die out pretty quickly if the Earth slowed down for some reason.

Have you ever wondered why our seasons happen at all? Whilst the equatorial regions have similar day lengths every day and a more or less constant temperature, the northern and southern hemispheres have opposing seasons. Whilst North America, Asia and Europe have their winter, South Americans, southern Africans and Antipodeans enjoy their summer, and vice versa. This brings stable growing conditions, which means planting, lambing and harvesting can be planned on an annual cycle, unless there are local disruptions such as a drought or unexpected flooding. Whilst events such as hurricanes or the failure of an annual rainfall can be disastrous for the people concerned, they serve to show just how reliable our weather system normally is.

The seasons and their moderate range are due to the stability of the Earth being held at a very helpful angle from the ecliptic (the plane in which the Earth orbits the Sun). This angle is currently 23°27' and it is decreasing at the rate of 48 seconds of arc per century and will decrease for several thousand years until it reaches 22°54', after which it will again increase to a maximum of around 24.5°. This changing angle is known as precession, a slow wobble of the Earth's axis in space, caused by the gravitational pull of the Moon – in harmony with the Sun – on the Earth's slight equatorial bulge. The Earth's axis traces out a cone in space, like a spinning top whose axis is not upright. This movement completes a cycle every 25,772 years.

This slow change of angle in relation to the Sun does cause climate changes at different latitudes, warming and cooling locations over millennia, but overall the Moon in particular holds the Earth in an embrace that brings a global balance of warmth and stability.

We enjoy the warmth of summer with its light evenings, but slowly the days grow shorter and the nights get longer. As

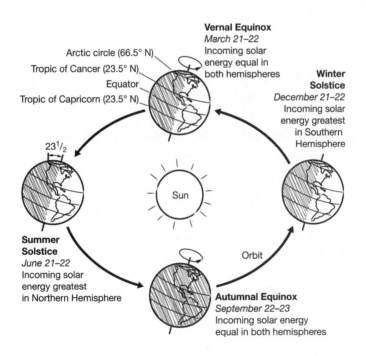

101

this happens, the average temperature each day begins to fall and much of the flora and fauna enters into a dormant state.

All of us who do not live on or near the equator are familiar with the pattern of the changing seasons and the effect that these cycles have on the way we live our lives. To our ancestors in northern parts of Europe, Asia and America, the onset of winter must have been a time of fear and doubt, whilst the first buds of spring would have been a merciful relief that signalled there would soon be fresh food to eat.

The planet Mercury is virtually 'upright' in relation to its orbit around the Sun and has equatorial temperatures that would boil lead, yet probes sent from Earth have shown that the polar regions of Mercury are constantly covered in ice. If the Earth were upright, life would be almost impossible across much of the planet, with extremes of temperature providing only a narrow band of sea and land suitable for the survival of mammals such as humans. Even then, the sea and air currents would move wildly between the boiling hot and the freezing cold zones, causing catastrophic weather conditions with regions of permanent rainfall and others with none at all. Hurricanes and tornadoes would ravage many areas and overall it seems extremely unlikely that higher life forms would ever develop on such a planet.

Our life-bringing seasons are due to the fact that the Earth is held at an angle relative to the equator of the Sun that produces a veritable incubator for life. That angle does not happen by itself. It is maintained by the presence of the Moon, which acts as a gigantic planetary stabilizer.

Whilst we all take our Moon for granted, it is a very strange object indeed.

# Jupiter the great protector

The existence of the gaseous giants of our own solar system has most certainly turned out to be extremely fortunate in the case of Earth, or at least the life developing upon it. Nobody doubts that in the earliest days of the solar system, not long after the planets had formed, the amount of loose debris in the solar system was much greater than it is today. One only has to observe the surface of the Moon to see just how many large rocks were once flying around on unstable orbits, ready to smash into any of the planets or their satellites. The reason we see so many craters on the Moon is because it has no atmosphere and therefore no surface erosion, so that ancient meteorite strikes still show in the form of craters. The Earth has suffered just as many impacts as the Moon in remote times. A few large meteorite craters are detectable on the Earth but many of the ancient ones have either weathered out, were destroyed by subsequent tectonic activity or may be hidden by vegetation or the oceans.

The most recent findings regarding the asteroid belt, that area of somewhat large rock and metal bodies that circles the Sun between the orbits of Mars and Jupiter, shows that impacts on the Earth from this part of space may have proved to be absolutely vital in terms of Earth's subsequent development. Asteroids have now been located that clearly contain water ice. Since nobody has ever been entirely sure where the Earth obtained its vast supply of water, the evidence of water in the asteroid belt has already convinced some scientists that they have found the answer. The great puzzle regarding Earth's water came about when it was realized that the very early Earth was far too hot to sustain any appreciable amount of water, which therefore must have appeared more recently. Some scientists suggest it was a host of meteor strikes upon the Earth, from the region of the asteroid belt which supplied the water that exists on the Earth today. However, this raises the question as to why the Moon has so little water. Surely, it should be covered with ice if meteors are the water-bringers?

Meanwhile, Jupiter is a true giant and even though it is mostly composed of gas its mass is greater than that of all the other planets put together. It may well have had sufficient gravitational pull to prevent what is now the asteroid belt from ever becoming a planet by preventing the normal process of accretion that would be expected to take place. A vast accumulation of so much debris occupying the same orbit would almost certainly lead to many collisions, some of which would have sent large quantities of rocks flying off at all imaginable angles, sped on their way by the force of the impacts in which they were involved. If those rocks were projected further into the solar system, some of them could, quite naturally, be expected to make contact with Mars, the Earth, Venus and Mercury. However, it seems that only the Earth, with its very particular conditions and placement in space, was able to retain the vast amounts of water that came into contact with the planets as a result of these early strikes.

It seems likely that eventually much of the smaller debris within the asteroid belt was thrown out of its orbit, either to collide with other planets, to be drawn into Jupiter or any of the other giant planets, or to be sent flying off into the depths of space. The asteroid belt still exists, of course, and there are still collisions, but probably not nearly as many as was the case much earlier in the history of the solar system.

After helping to seed the Earth with the necessary water that would eventually allow life to develop, the huge Jupiter then began to help our planet in a totally different way. As already mentioned, the solar system contains objects other than the planets and the asteroids. The most important of these are the comets: large accretions of rock and ice, which are often called 'dirty snowballs'. They have extremely elliptical orbits, which take them far out to the furthest reaches of the solar system before they turn and return, often to do a tight turn around the Sun before disappearing off into the blackness of space again. As they approach the Sun, comets warm up and begin to leave long trails of water vapour and dust behind them. In historical times the appearance of a comet in the night sky was considered a harbinger of bad fortune and, although the people living then had no idea, in some cases their foreboding could have been correct.

It stands to reason that any object with such a strange orbit as that of the average comet will, at some stage on each of its journeys around the Sun, have had to cross the path of the Earth. Of course the Earth itself has a very long journey each year, so the chances of a comet coming close enough to the Earth to be attracted by its gravitational pull are quite low, but there are many comets and some of them have distinctly rogue orbits.

Back in the early 1990s two scientists, Eugene and Carolyn Shoemaker, discovered a new comet, which was given the designation 'Shoemaker–Levy 9'. It didn't take long to work out that this particular comet had a highly eccentric orbit and one that estimations showed would take it extremely close to Jupiter. In 1992 the comet did indeed pass near to the giant planet's surface and the massive gravitational tug ripped the comet into at least 21 separate fragments. Some of these

105

chunks collided with Jupiter on its next circuit between 16 July and 22 July 1994. The resulting explosions were colossal.

The collision of the fragments of Shoemaker–Levy 9 with Jupiter was observed by people all over the world. This was the first time in recorded history that such a phenomenon had been seen. Quite understandably this got scientists thinking about Jupiter's significance with regard to debris that enters our solar system and it became known in some circles as the 'comet catcher'. But this giant of a planet is far from alone in its ability to capture and destroy many of the wandering bodies within the solar system that might ultimately make contact with the Earth. Second only to Jupiter in terms of its mass and therefore its gravitational pull is the planet Saturn, closely followed by Uranus and Neptune. In other words we have not one sentinel but four, all lying between the orbit of the Earth and the far reaches of the solar system.

It has never been suggested that this wonderful level of protection that the supergiants offer the Earth is anything more than a happy coincidence, and it is explained as being part of the cure-all theory known as the anthropic principle. Basically, the argument is that these planets have to save us from regular bombardment or we would not be here to observe the fact. Certainly it seems unlikely that life more complex than the amoebae would evolve if gigantic global fireballs struck the Earth with any regularity.

## Are there alien worlds?

In January 2011 NASA announced that it had identified its first genuinely Earth-like planet, a rocky sphere with a diameter 1.4 times that of our own planet, orbiting a star designated as Kepler–10.

Although it is 560 light years from Earth, the scientists involved had spotted the relatively small planet by measuring the minute dips in light as the planet passed in front of its star, or sun. Geoff Marcy, a planet-hunting astronomer at the University of California, described Kepler–10b as 'a planetary missing link, a bridge between the gas giant planets we've been finding and the Earth itself'.

However, whilst Kepler–10b does seem to have an Earth-like size, it is also a distinctly hellish place. Instead of occupying a temperate orbit in the 'habitable zone' around its sun (the area around a star where water has the possibility of remaining liquid), it is just a few million miles out from its sun. Consequently, it has an average surface temperature of around 1,300°C and a density close to that of iron. Kepler–10b has no possibility of giving rise to life as we would recognize it.

Almost all the planets found around other stars have been similarly disappointing. Most are massively too hot and some are frozen solid. The bad news is that of the 500 or so planets found beyond our own star system, all are barren lumps of space debris. And this fact is causing some astronomers to rethink all their assumptions about the likelihood of ever finding life beyond our own little planet.

'The new information we are getting suggests we could effectively be alone in the universe. There are very few solar systems or planets like ours,' said Howard Smith, a senior astrophysicist at Harvard University. 'It means it is highly unlikely there are any planets with intelligent life close enough for us to make contact.'

Later the same year, in December 2011, the idea that intelligent life might exist elsewhere in the universe appeared to take a leap forward. A newly discovered planet had been found that could, according to Alan Boss of the Carnegie Institution for Science, very well contain continental features where it was possible for some kind of human-like – or dolphin-like – life forms to have evolved. NASA announced that its Kepler space telescope confirmed the first planet orbiting a star in its 'habitable zone' – the region where liquid water could theoretically exist on a planet's surface. Located some 600 light years away, Kepler-22b is about 2.4 times the radius of Earth but scientists have no idea of its mass and do not know if it has a rocky, gaseous or liquid composition.

If it is made of rock, as some speculate, Dr Boss says it might look something like our own Earth and it might have a fair amount of water on it as well. The planet's host star belongs to the same class as our Sun, called G-type, although it is slightly smaller and cooler. Dr Boss said, that if it is rock, had water and an atmosphere similar to ours, Kepler-22b's surface temperature would be close to 72°F, 'like a rather pleasant day on Earth, a nice spring day'.

Really? The enthusiasm to find some indication that we are not alone in the cosmos causes what can be politely called 'undue optimism'. Claims that this distant planet, of which we know so little, might have produced higher life forms are utterly baseless. It would be about as sensible to spot a new island in the South Pacific by distant radar and guess that it might independently have evolved camels.

The team involved in identifying Kepler-22b must be congratulated on some excellent work. They have chosen to use 'equilibrium temperature' because it is something they know how to calculate, but it requires knowledge of the planetary albedo (the fraction of incoming light being absorbed by the planet), and they have to assume that a greenhouse effect 'like the Earth's' exists to bring the temperature to the comfortable 72°F (22°C). As a number of informed commentators have pointed out, their claim of temperature does not even justify the term 'estimate' – it is just a statement of what this planet would be like if it is like the Earth. There are countless other possibilities, which would result in entirely different temperature values.

The fact that this planet does not have a large moon to stabilize its tilt and create seasons like the Earth makes seasons impossible. This planet is far too large to be truly Earth-like and, until scientists get some atmospheric measurements, it is impossible to know what the surface temperature is. The fact is, it could have a runaway greenhouse effect, and therefore be as life-unfriendly as lead-boiling Venus, or it might just be a ball of gas.

Dr Boss's claim about the possible temperature is particularly strange when one considers the size of this planet. If it is made of rock, as is hoped, it would probably have a gravity nearly 14 times greater than that of the Earth, making it unlikely that any mobile creature could evolve a mineral skeletal structure to lift itself off the ground. It would also mean that an atmosphere like ours would have a pressure of around 200 pounds per square inch at sea level, which means that water could not evaporate in normal-strength sunlight. A high-pressure atmosphere causes a rise in the temperature at which water boils, and on the planet there would be no clouds and no rain. The sea would be near flat and the air dry as a bone. A strange spring day indeed!

It seems that our planet – and our planet alone – is a perfect size and mass to produce advanced life as we know it. The bottom line is that our 'blue planet' enjoys too many special qualities for there to be many, perhaps any, other Earths across the cosmos – as unimaginably vast as it is.

There is a well-known theorem which states that a monkey hitting keys at random on a typewriter keyboard for an infinite amount of time will eventually type the complete works of William Shakespeare. The probability of a monkey typing even one Shakespeare play is so tiny that the chance of it occurring at all is 100,000 orders of magnitude longer than the age of the universe. The probability is massively in favour of there only being one *Romeo and Juliet*.

I suggest that the Earth is likely to be the only 'Shakespeare play' in the entire cosmos. We may well be alone – which brings great responsibility.

# Chapter 10

# THE POWER OF NUMBERS

'Pure mathematics is, in its way, the poetry
of logical ideas.'

*Albert Einstein*

Throughout this book there have been many numbers used to describe the mass of objects, their length, volume, speed and pressure. Everything requires numbers to describe it and those numbers relate to a system of units. A wide variety of units has been invented to measure things; from the curie to the carat or the folio to the fathom, we have specialized units to make comparisons and describe quantities.

In our modern world, numeracy is next to godliness.

Unfortunately, there is a great deal of confusion because of competing systems of measurement, which appear to have come from different historical roots. And whilst most units work well enough in their area of application, they don't often integrate with other systems.

Surely, if God did create the universe and the myriad of complex rules for the laws of physics, there must be a better way of making measurements work meaningfully? Could there be a universal 'true' system of metrology (the science of measuring) in our world?

## The great metrology challenge

Shortly after he was appointed US Secretary of State, Thomas Jefferson was asked by the House of Representatives in November 1789 to devise a new system of units of measurement for the USA. On 4 July 1790, he presented his report 'A Plan for Establishing Uniformity in the Coinage, Weights and Measures of the United States'.

Jefferson submitted two proposals: a decimal system and a related non-decimal one. Both had great merit, but change is difficult and Jefferson's proposals were never implemented. The USA stayed with the old-fashioned foot, the mile, the pound and a revised version of the pint and the gallon.

All these old units had come from England and are believed to have had their origin in disparate, inaccurate estimates of average body parts or handy beer-swilling volumes. How inappropriate for the modern age – at least the metric system was based on a logical subdivision of the Earth's polar circumference.

Although England is the country that produced the units used in the modern USA, things have changed in England and the rest of the United Kingdom. Today, measurement systems have become even more confusing. I am English, so I know this fact only too well.

Consider this: my wife Caroline and I get in my car to drive to a favourite spot where we can walk to a lovely little country pub. The car is built using *millimetres* and its engine is specified in *cubic centimetres*. I fill it with fuel by the *litre*, drive for several *minutes* at 30 *miles per hour* to my destination – the computer keeping track of fuel consumption in *miles to the gallon*. I park the car next to the cricket pitch (one *chain* long) and we follow the footpath across *acres* of farmland to the pub signposted in *metres*, where I order a *pint* of beer for myself and a 175-*millilitre* glass of wine for Caroline.

Oh, and the compass bearing from the car was 19° (*degrees*) west of north (or 19/360th of the circle around me). And the temperature was a pleasant 21°*Celsius* – or 70°*Fahrenheit* if you prefer. The altitude was 780 *feet* and the air pressure was 1008 *millibars*.

There is only one system in use globally for geometry and another for time. Whilst there are 360 degrees to a circle there are 60 seconds to a minute and 60 minutes to the hour – and therefore 3,600 seconds in an hour. Both of these systems are connected and have come down to us from the Sumerian culture that existed in what is now Iraq and Kuwait around 5,000 years ago. This civilization originally had a standard unit equal to 12 double-hours in a day before they were eventually turned into the current 24 hours.

Not every country is so perfectly confused as my homeland, where measurements – other than time/geometry – are a mixture of the traditional English (or Imperial units) and the modern metric system. According to the standard explanation, the Imperial system was first defined in the British Weights and Measures Act of 1824, which drew together and formalized a wide range of disparate units that had been used in England and the rest of the British Isles from time immemorial. They include measures of length, area, weight, capacity and more.

The basic units of length are the inch, foot and the yard
– with 12 inches to the foot and 36 inches to the yard. Some
believe the yard was derived from the double cubit, others
suggest that it is the length of an average stride – and some
believe the measure was the distance between the tip of
anyone's nose to the end of their thumb, a rough-and-ready
tradesman's unit to dispense lengths of cloth.

Having been at school in England during the 1950s
and 1960s, I was taught the full range of apparently crazy
measures. The basic unit of British currency was, as it still
is, the pound sterling, but instead of being subdivided into a
neat 100 pence, back then there were 4 farthings to a penny,
12 pennies to a shilling, 2 shillings to the florin, 5 shillings
to the crown and a total of 240 pennies to the pound.
There were coins of many values, including the farthing
until the end of 1960. That meant that it was possible to
have 960 bronze coins in your pocket to make up just one
pound. And just to confuse a little more, luxury items were
normally advertised for sale in guineas, which was a pound
and a shilling (equal to 1,008 bronze farthings, which would
have weighed nearly half a stone.

These coinage values appear to have much in common
with the Sumerian units of geometry and time, in which
numbers 12 and 36 are important. For example, 360 pennies
was equal to 1.5 pounds sterling.

The one significant advantage that the old British system
of coinage had over the modern decimal system was that it
was possible to have exact values for thirds and two thirds of
a pound as well as halves and quarters. I remember that 13
shillings and four pence was two thirds of a pound, whereas
today the closest one can get is 66 pence.

A wide range of old English units of measure of one kind or another still remain in use, such as the acre and the pint, but many that I remember from my childhood have largely disappeared. How I recall the 'rod' with curious affection, because it was also called a pole or a perch. It mattered not to my teachers that no one in real life still used this unit – and there were no rulers or tape measures delineated in these arcane divisions – they just had to be learned. My examiners required me to know that this unit was a quarter of a chain and that the otherwise illogical unit of an agricultural acre could be defined as land that was 4 rods wide and 40 rods long.

Then, among these archaic, yet oh so recent measures, sit such apparently disparate concepts as the ancient bushel, the furlong, the hundredweight and the fathom.

These units are thought to be a random collection of values drawn together in a ludicrously eccentric manner. The poet G K Chesterton captured the spirit of the lunacy when he wrote the first verse of 'The Rolling English Road':

Before the Romans came to Rye or out of Severn strode,
The rolling English drunkard made the rolling English
    road.
A reeling road, a rolling road, that rambles round the
    shire,
And after him the parson ran, the sexton and the squire;
A merry road, a mazy road, such as we did tread
The night we went to Birmingham by way of Beachy
    Head.

It is generally believed that these various old units started with rough-and-ready measures, slowly becoming more and more defined as the needs of commerce required.

The metric system was apparently devised by the French following their revolution, but even that improvement lacks any great thought behind it. The only reality is that the metre was defined as 1/40-millionth of the polar circumference of the Earth. The rest of the metric system stemmed from that unit of length.

## A metrology competition

One open-minded Oxford-educated engineer, Edmund Six-smith, who has shown a great deal of interest in the researches carried out by Alan Butler and myself, came up with the idea of throwing out a challenge. It might be, he suggested, time for someone to revisit Thomas Jefferson's task and invent a much more sensible integrated system of measurements – with some deep-seated natural logic behind it. Edmund decided that entries should not be confined to length and weight but must extend to angle and any other units that entrants care to define within their proposed system.

The requirement was to devise an ingenious new system of measurement that integrates units of time with temperature, mass, volume, length, capacity and angle – all of which should be easy to reconstruct by anyone washed up on a desert island without any tools or gauges. They also had to be meaningful to the Earth, in the way that the metre is geodetic because it has an integer relationship with the planet's polar circumference. Ideally, it would also have an integer relationship with the circumference of the Sun and the Moon.

Now that is what I call a challenge!

The judging criteria for assessing the proposed systems was to have included the question: can you *calibrate* your unit of length with universally available materials and a simple method (the desert island test)? An accuracy of one part in 500 was the target for unaided reconstruction anywhere on the planet.

A tough call? It certainly seems so.

Edmund was unable to persuade any publication to run this competition because it was considered to be utterly impossible and therefore pointless. How could anyone create measurement units, based on the Earth, Moon and Sun that were fully interconnected and covered everything from angles to temperature to mass in an intuitive and harmonious way, they asked?

It does seem impossible, yet an answer to this challenge has been successfully demonstrated. It makes a truly giant leap forward for humankind.

## The greatest system of measurements ever!

At the heart of this winning 'uber-system' is the value 366. Let us call this new approach to measures the 'EMS' system, with EMS standing for 'Earth–Moon–Sun'.

The value of 366 was chosen because it is probably the most fundamental number associated with our planet: the Earth makes 366 complete rotations on its axis for each orbit of the Sun.

Whilst there are 365 whole days (mean solar days) in a normal year, the planet actually turns once more, but it is not noticed because our journey around the Sun appears to take one day off the total. (If you were to ignore your calendar and watch any star as it rises, it would do so 366 times between two consecutive winter solstices, for example.)

The path that the Earth scribes on its annual route around the Sun is taken by this system to be the most fundamental of all circles. And each full rotation of our planet on that journey is taken to represent one degree.

Next, these EMS degrees are divided into six minutes of arc and each of those minutes into 60 seconds. Each turn of the Earth represents 240 EMS seconds of arc of the planet's orbit around the sun.

The next step for the new system was to apply the 366 degrees to subdivide the Earth's polar circumference. There are a number of different estimates for this measurement, ranging between 39,941 and 40,010 kilometres, but it is taken here as 40,009,153m, as provided by Koordinaten, a German company that specializes in large distance calculations.*

The circumference of the Earth is divided and subdivided as follows:

Into 366 degrees = 109,314m

Each degree is divided into six minutes = 18,219m

Each minute is divided into 60 seconds = 303.656m

Each second of arc on the Earth's surface is then divided again into 366 subdivisions, giving a unit of length equal to 82.966cm.

---

* See www.koordinaten.de/english/informations/earth.shtml

This length is taken as the fundamental unit of the EMS system. Let us call it a 'metron' – the ancient Greek word for 'measure'.

The metron and the 366-geometry behind it are indeed related to the Earth's polar circumference, but how does it have any relationship with the Moon and the Sun?

The Moon is estimated to have a circumference of 10,917km, which equates to 13,158,402 metrons. This breaks down as follows:

Moon's circumference = 13,158,402 metrons
One EMS degree       = 35,951 metrons
One EMS minute       = 5,992 metrons
One EMS second       = 100 metrons

The Sun's circumference is harder to identify but NASA takes it to be 4,373,096km, which gives the following result:

Sun's circumference = 5,270,913 metrons
One EMS degree      = 14,401,404 metrons
One EMS minute      = 240,023 metrons
One EMS second      = 40,004 metrons

So, the Earth has 366 metrons to a second of arc, the Moon has 100 metrons and the Sun 40,000 metrons. This system therefore has a beautiful integer relationship with them all.

A further neatness for this new measurement system is that the Moon and the Sun both appear to be the same size as each other in the sky when viewed from the surface of the Earth. Both are half an EMS degree wide, so together they account for one degree. With a standard degree they are a fairly close fit, but this 366-based degree makes it as perfect as it can get.

The next unit to create is one to define capacity. This is done using exactly the same principle that is applied for the metric system, where a cube is made with sides one tenth of a metre. The water this cube holds is called a litre and the weight of the water is called a kilogramme. In the case of the EMS system, a cube is made with sides that are one tenth of a metron and it is filled with water. This gives a result of 571 grammes, which we can call a pint – because it is; for all practical purposes it is an Imperial pint, as defined by the Exchequer in London in 1601, to an accuracy better than one part in 5,000. (This is the 20-fluid-ounce pint as opposed to the newer American version of 16 fluid ounces.)

If each of the sides of the cube is doubled, the capacity increases to one Imperial gallon.

When it comes to weight, the new standard unit is established by carefully filling the one-tenth metron cube to the brim with any non-polished grain such as wheat or barley. This can be called a pound weight – because it is a standard pound of 16 ounces. Double the sides of the cube and it weighs a bushel.

Neither the gallon nor the bushel are thought to have any cube relationship with their respective base unit, let alone each other, and have a connection to the physical Earth, Moon and Sun.

The Imperial pound, which suddenly makes itself part of a coherent system, is made up of 16 subdivisions called ounces. Very strangely, a cube that holds distilled water weighing 1,000oz will have sides precisely one Imperial foot (or 12in) in length. This very bizarre relationship between an Imperial unit of weight and another of length simply should not exist. This extreme oddity was recognized and reported upon by the brilliant gentleman-scientist Thomas Jefferson, who went on to become the third president of the USA.

But the amazing totality of this new EMS system goes much deeper.

The mass of the Earth is now accepted as an arbitrary-sounding $5.9763 \times 10^{24}$kg* and, when converted into Imperial (known as avoirdupois) pounds, comes to a figure of $1.31754 \times 10^{25}$lb. If the globe of the Earth is divided up into 366 parts to produce segments (like those of an orange) that are one EMS degree across, each degree will weigh 35,998,360,655, 737,704,918,033lb. This sounds rather unimpressive, but if each of these degree segments is subdivided into 360 seconds of arc, each unit would be 366 metrons wide at the equator. So a one-second slice of the planet under this new system would weigh an astonishingly neat 100,000,000,000,000,000,000lb (100 million, trillion pounds).

How can it be that a brand new 'uber-system' of measurements can have such a beautifully neat relationship with the Earth? And, even more perplexingly, how come it is the Imperial pint and the pound behind it all; units whose origins are lost to human memory?

The EMS system can now turn to the subject of temperature.

## Hot and very cold

When applied to temperature measurement this new approach makes the modern Celsius and Fahrenheit scales look distinctly amateur. In 1724 German physicist Daniel

---

* New York Public Library, *Service Desk Reference*, Macmillan, New York, 1995

Fahrenheit designed a scale based on pure water freezing at 32° and boiling at 212° (at 1 bar atmospheric pressure). A little later, in 1742, Swedish astronomer Anders Celsius created a rather more simple relationship between freezing and boiling points by adopting 0° for freezing water and 100° for boiling water. In both scales the most universally meaningful point of temperature, that of absolute zero (the coldest that anything can be), has an arbitrary value of −460° and −273° respectively.

The EMS system based on 366 produces a far more beautiful result. Taking the freezing point of distilled water as zero and the boiling point of water at sea level to be 366°, absolute zero comes in at a distinguished −1000°. Far more elegant than its competitors:

| System | Boiling point | Freezing | Absolute zero |
|---|---|---|---|
| Fahrenheit | 212° | 32° | −460° |
| Celsius | 100° | 0° | −273° |
| EMS | 366° | 0° | −1000° |

# A new (yet old) approach to music

At its equator the Earth turns through one EMS second of arc (366 metrons) in a period of time that can be called 'an EMS second of time' – equal to 0.6557 modern seconds. A musical note with a frequency of 366 cycles for every EMS second of time is in tune with the turning Earth because there is one vibration for every metron of planetary turn at the equator.

In standard terms, a frequency of 366 cycles per EMS second would be 558Hz, which places such a note a fraction above C5 sharp in modern concert tuning.

Any musical instrument can be tuned to this primary note. Because all the notes in a scale are harmonious and therefore have a mathematical relationship with the starting, or 'root', note, it would follow that any piece of music played in this revised C sharp would enjoy a mathematical relationship with the turning Earth, both in terms of the planet's dimensions and its spin.

Strangely, this adjusted scale is found in the traditional instruments of many older cultures, from the music of the Aboriginal Australians to the indigenous peoples of South America. Indeed, aboriginal peoples designate this EMS version of C sharp as representative of the Earth.

## The desert island test

Part of the challenge issued by Edmund Sixsmith was that the new system had to be more than a convention, in that it had to come from nature. The test of this aspect was that a man or woman with the appropriate knowledge should be able to re-create the identified units without any tools.

So imagine a sailor washed up on a desert island. Let's call him Crusoe. Our shipwrecked sailor has to make his tools from items around him. First, Crusoe has to find some natural twine – such as a liana, the climbing vine found throughout tropical rainforests that Tarzan famously uses to swing from tree to tree. These plants can be very long indeed, but Crusoe only needs relatively short bits. Or he can make some twine by twisting natural fibres together. Then he must find four straight sticks roughly twice his own height, a sharp rock for cutting, an empty coconut shell (or similar) and a few handfuls of natural clay.

Crusoe knows what to do. Having selected his sticks, cut his rope and found some natural clay, he looks for an area of his island that is a decent size, flat and reasonably level with a clear horizon, ideally looking out to sea in an approximate north or south direction. Then he selects a straight stick to use as a laying-out device and cuts it neatly to a usable length – about the span of an outstretched hand would be ideal, but it can be any convenient length. Next, he puts another short stick vertically in the ground and ties the rope to it before measuring out 233 lengths of his hand-length stick along the rope stretched out straight and pointing towards the sea. He then places another small stick vertically in the middle of the measured rope (between the 116th and 117th points). Then he erects two tall sticks at the end of the rope nearest to the sea, so that they have a gap between them that is exactly two hand-length sticks wide.

This complicated-sounding, but actually very simple, procedure has created a gap that, when viewed from the centre stick, gives a section of the horizon that is one 366th of the circle of the Earth.

Crusoe knows that he must now adjust the angle of his sticks so that the stars behind the stick appear to travel horizontally across the gap. Then Crusoe needs to build a clock to time the stars. To modern ears this sounds like a complete impossibility, because of the assumed need for cogs and complex mechanical structures. But all that our shipwrecked friend needs is a pendulum, as the other parts of

*Using a length of twine and a few sticks is enough to create a circle that divides the horizon into 366 equal parts. The viewer places their head at the centre point to time the passage of Venus using a pendulum that swings at the rate of 366 times whilst the planet remains in view between two sticks marking the division of the horizon.*

a clock (the spring, cogs, hands and face) are just a means of automating timekeeping and making it easy to read. Crusoe requires only a hand-clock, which he makes by rolling a small ball of clay with a short length of twine threaded through it to form a pendulum.

Swinging his pendulum gently from his fingertips Crusoe sends the weight of clay arcing from side to side at a fixed rate. It does not matter how much energy he puts into the swing, because the time it takes the weight to get from one side to the other is determined almost entirely by the length of the cord.* Swing harder and the increased energy goes into making the ball of clay scribe a larger arc – but the time between extremities remains the same. The only way to change the time taken to make a beat (one side to the other) is to shorten or lengthen the cord.

Crusoe can now time a star passing across the gap, or even better he can use the very bright 'Evening Star', which is the planet Venus at certain times of the year. He stands at the centre point of the rope circle and waits for Venus to disappear behind the first stick. At the moment the planet becomes eclipsed, he swings his pendulum and counts the number of beats before it disappears behind the second stick. His task is to adjust the length of the cord until he has exactly 366 beats whilst Venus is visible in its transit across the gap. He knows the approximate length he is looking for so the trial-and-error technique will not take too long.

Through this technique Crusoe has divided the sky into 366 equal parts and measured 366 beats that happen as Venus or the star passes across the gap. This means he has identified 1/366th part of one revolution of the Earth and created a pendulum that beats at 366 times during that time.

There are 86,400 seconds in a mean solar day, but there are 236 seconds less in a single rotation of the Earth, known as a sidereal day (the length of time that it takes for a star to return to its starting point in the sky on two consecutive evenings).† It follows that the 366 measured beats fitted into a time period of just under 235.5 seconds.

---

* Altitude, atmospheric pressure and latitude can have a tiny effect but can be ignored for all practical purposes.
† The difference comes about because of the Earth's orbit around

*Venus transiting between the poles (for accuracy the poles have to be adjusted to ensure that the planet travels at 90 degrees to the poles).*

Crusoe now takes the length of his pendulum and carefully scribes a circle using the fulcrum as the centre and the middle of the clay ball to delineate the circumference. He knows that the diameter of that circle is the key to everything – it is 82.966cm across and it is therefore a metron.

As he looks towards the north he is reminded that this unit he has just re-created is very special in terms of Earth geometry. Although he has made this unit by measuring the eastwards rotation of the planet it has special qualities for the polar circumference as well.

---

the Sun, which adds 236 seconds to the time between two noons. The actual spin of the Earth is the sidereal or star day.

Crusoe now cuts a stick that is exactly the diameter of the circle he has just scribed. He now has a metron rule.

Armed with his star-length (the metron), taken from nature by measuring the turning of the Earth, Crusoe can set about making all kinds of other units to measure weight, distance and capacity. Firstly, he cuts a stick to make it one tenth of his metron rule, then he rolls out flat sheets of clay using a smooth log as a rolling pin. He cuts these into squares so he can fix five pieces together such that he has an open-topped cube with internal sides the length of his small measure-stick. He fills this with water to the brim. Because he has the appropriate knowledge, Crusoe knows his clay cube now holds one Imperial pint. If he has been totally accurate in his manufacturing process, so will his pint be accurate.

He can then transfer the water to another container, such as a coconut shell, and mark the water level on the sides to create a pint-measuring jug for future use.

Then he places seeds from any available grass plant into his clay cube and when filled level he has a pound weight. If Crusoe was bored and looking for something to do he could make some accurate units of length as well. He knows there are 20fl oz to an Imperial pint,* so 50 of his cubes of water would weigh 1,000oz. It would take quite an effort but Crusoe could build a large cube holding the contents of 50 of his pint cubes and the internal length of one side will be a foot long. Three lengths would be a yard, and 1,760 of these would be a mile.

---

* The USA changed its pint to 16fl oz (fluid ounces) to match the number of ounces in a pound. This 'improvement' dislocated their fluid measures from the ancient pattern.

But there is more. Crusoe can return to his turning-Earth-viewer the next day and adjust his pendulum so that it beats 236 times whilst Venus passes across his predetermined gap. Because Crusoe has been trained in the art of natural measurements he knows that each beat will take exactly one second and the pendulum is a near-perfect metre long. From this he can measure out kilometres and make a cube of one tenth of a metre to create kilogrammes and litres.

## God's units?

So, here is a system that fully integrates time, length, volume, weight, temperature and angles, and makes them geodetic.

The really odd thing here is that the units produced are not some clever new invention; they are the same ones that have been used for many centuries in England – or France in the case of the metric units.

What is even stranger is that these old units of length, mass, capacity and time are supposed to have no relationship to each other. And none of these units is known to have any correlation with the turning of the Earth.

What is going on? Where has this brilliant system come from?

The answer is that the metron and the 366-based EMS system are older than history itself. It turns out that all these units – from the second of time to the pound, the pint, the gallon, the yard, the mile, the kilo, the metre and the rest – were first devised in the distant past. The memory of their origin became lost through the breakdown of civilizations and the idea arose that they were just old, rough measures that had evolved in an unplanned way. This mist of the centuries caused the knowledge that they were the result of pure observational astronomy to be completely lost.

# Chapter 11

# A STONE AGE MYSTERY

'I believe we are a species with amnesia, I think we have forgotten our roots and our origins.'

*Graham Hancock*

A system that produces new units based on the harmony of the Earth and also delivers up a gateway to reproduce a range of existing, apparently unrelated, units is staggering. But what connection does it have with the possibility of there being a creator God – and which genius came up with this miraculous EMS system that uses the physical realities of the Sun, Moon and Earth to underpin all of the main measurement units used in the world today?

The possibility of a connection with God will become clear shortly, but the identity of the people who devised this EMS system is very strange indeed. It was not created by a team of mathematicians from the Massachusetts Institute of Technology, nor was it the inspiration of some brilliant Nobel Prize-winning physicist. It was actually brought to the world by some unknown individuals who lived 5,500 years ago in the Late Stone Age!

# The scientists from prehistory

I became interested in the Late Neolithic period of the British Isles back in 1997, after I had been contacted by a researcher and writer called Alan Butler. Alan had read my first book, *The Hiram Key*, and felt that in some way we were on a similar path. With a background in engineering and a good knowledge of astronomy, Alan had noticed that parts of the ancient world had used a year of 366 days, which is the number of sidereal (star) days in one orbit of the Sun. He had, as I said earlier, been particularly interested in an artefact known as the Phaistos Disc, a 4,000-year-old disc of fired clay from the Minoan palace of Phaistos on the Greek island of Crete. It is about 6in (15cm) in diameter and covered on both sides with a spiral of stamped symbols, which Alan determined was a perpetual calendar based on 366 days per year.

Alan had also noticed that the unit of measure used to build the Minoan palaces in ancient times had an apparent connection to the earlier structures in the British Isles. The Minoan Foot had been identified by Canadian archaeologist J Walter Graham as being 30.36cm – which had a connection to a unit called the 'Megalithic Yard'.

The Megalithic Yard is a unit of measure that was, it is claimed, used by the builders of prehistoric stone structures such as Stonehenge. It was identified by Alexander Thom, a distinguished professor of engineering at the University of Oxford, who dedicated almost half a century to surveying Stone Age sites in the British Isles and Brittany in western France. As a young man during the early 1930s Alexander Thom had visited a number of prehistoric stone structures near to his home in Scotland. He had admired the way so many of the giant stones had survived the weathering of thousands of years and he came to the conclusion that the builders of these structures had been engineers – just like himself.

Whilst archaeology is generally more concerned with digging up scraps of cultural remnants and attempting to second-guess how these prehistoric builders lived, Thom set about trying to understand their engineering minds. It became clear to him that most, if not all, of the sites he studied had astronomical alignments with stars, the Moon and the Sun. He would study the layout of each site and build a picture in his mind of what he thought their plan had been. He would then create his own solution to the assumed problem. Having drawn up his own design, he then compared it to the stones he could see to gain an insight into its purpose, which gave him the ability to often predict the location of missing stones, which allowed him to locate the socket hole that confirmed his expectation.

Thom's first survey was at a site known as Callanish on the Isle of Lewis in the Hebrides off the west coast of Scotland. This complex of standing stones revealed many astronomical alignments and is today often referred to as a 'Moon temple'.

Thom developed his own, new, statistical technique to establish the relative positions of the stones and, over time, something spectacularly unusual emerged from the amassed data. The prehistoric builders had manufactured these structures working with a standard unit of measurement across a huge area of thousands of square miles, from the islands off northern Scotland down to Brittany on the Atlantic coast of France.

It was utterly amazing that these supposedly primitive people could have had a universal convention for a unit of length, yet Thom was eventually able to describe the supreme accuracy of a unit he called the Megalithic Yard. This was no approximate measure taken from paces or body parts; it was equal to 2.722ft +/− 0.002ft (82.97cm +/− 0.06mm). That means that these Stone Age engineers were placing their huge stones, many weighing tens of tons, to an accuracy of the width of a couple of human hairs. That is a level of exactitude more common to watchmakers rather than modern builders. (The Megalithic Yard is, of course, the same as the 'metron' explained in the previous chapter.)

Thom was also able to demonstrate that this unit was frequently used in its double- and half-forms as well as being broken down, for use in design work, into 40 sub-units that he designated 'Megalithic Inches'.

Such a breakthrough in the understanding of the abilities of people in the British Neolithic period should have changed all the existing preconceptions. Most archaeologists at the time responded by refuting the finding on the basis that the idea that there was an ancient unit of measurement that was more accurate than a modern measuring tape was absurd. Thom admitted that he could not suggest how it could have been achieved but he stood by his evidence that simply said it very clearly 'had' been done. As a mathematician and an engineer he saw it as his role to report what was testably true about these very ancient structures – but it was not within his remit to explain how or why these people had done it.

Although a few archaeologists are highly scientific, using highly advanced methods of investigation and analysis, many – perhaps most – spend their time digging up artefacts and then creating elaborate explanations for their findings. Archaeology has shown itself to be a closed discipline, which is why all outsiders, however distinguished in their own field, are shunned. Highly informed findings and conclusions by non-archaeologists are almost always ignored.

A good example is my friend Gordon Freeman, a retired professor who was previously chairman of the University of Alberta's Physical and Theoretical Chemistry Department. He holds an MA from the University of Saskatchewan, a PhD from McGill University and a DPhil from the University of Oxford. Gordon has published over 450 papers on chemistry, physics and various other subjects. He is also a superb archaeologist – albeit an amateur one (in the same sense that Alexander Thom was an amateur).

Gordon has spent over 30 years studying stone structures in his native Canada and in Europe. He has published claims that Native North American peoples used a series of stones and rocks, stretching over 12 square miles, as a calendar to mark the changing of seasons and the phases of the lunar cycle more than 5,000 years ago. Naturally this assertion has not gone down well with the archeological establishment, which sees its authority as being threatened by such 'intrusions'. A Canadian TV station interviewed two archaeologists when Gordon's book was published about his discovery of a 'Canadian Stonehenge'. They laughed and told the reporter that it was all rubbish that could be safely ignored. The reporter then asked them if they had read the book or studied Professor Freeman's findings. They replied, without any apparent embarrassment at the possibility of branding themselves complete fools, that they had not read any of Gordon Freeman's work.

Even today Thom's Megalithic Yard is largely shunned by the archaeological establishment, where hard science tends to be ignored in favour of hunches and pontifications by supposed luminaries. There is a widespread fallacy that somehow Alexander Thom's unit has long ago been 'shown to be a mistake'. I have heard it said many times that the Megalithic Yard has been 'proven not to exist'. This claim is untrue – and scientifically absurd, as it is impossible to prove a negative. The fact is that whilst most archaeologists do not believe that Thom's statistical analysis was correct, the mathematics says the unit did exist.

Just as some religious people who believe that their scriptures give a better account of events than the theory of evolution have a right to their ideas, archaeologists can prefer their traditional accounts to Thom's evidence. But their objections cannot be called science!

Back in 1998, with Alan Butler I set about the task of trying to establish whether Thom could be shown to be correct concerning his Megalithic Yard. Our starting assumption was that prehistoric builders would have been likely to take a measurement from nature as their standard, rather than adopting an abstract and meaningless length. Indeed, this seemed very likely because the consistent accuracy that Thom found across thousands of years and tens of thousands of square miles precluded the possibility of mass-produced measuring sticks. The universal accuracy of the Megalithic Yard strongly suggested that it was being repeatedly re-created from something in nature rather than merely copied. This proved to be the case.

We were to discover that Thom's Megalithic Yard is a perfect geodetic unit, in that it has a whole-number (integer) relationship with the Earth's polar circumference. We found that these early Megalithic builders viewed a circle as having 366 degrees rather than the 360 degrees that we use today. We realized that there really should be 366 degrees in a circle for the very good reason that there are 366 rotations of the Earth in one orbit of the Sun – the most fundamental of all circles in human existence.

Any sky-watcher will quickly realize that the field of stars passes over his or her head in two ways – once each day and once each year. The first is due to the Earth rotating once on its axis before any given star returns to its starting point, and the second is because of our planet's orbit around the Sun once between successive winter (or summer) solstices. Stone Age sky-watchers could not help noticing that there were 366 of the daily star movements in a great circle to one even bigger circle every complete cycle of the seasons.

As already stated, one solar orbit is a year but there is very slight difference between the number of rotations of the planet and the 365¼ days in a year. A sidereal day easily is appreciated by observing a star returning to the same point in the heavens on two consecutive nights. This rotational day is 236 seconds shorter than a mean solar day. Over the course of a year there is exactly one mean solar day difference (86,400 seconds).

## Wheels within wheels

Early cultures frequently took their lead from nature and they were fond of 'wheels within wheels'. If the circle of the heavens had 366 parts, why should every circle not follow the same rule? The ancient principle was 'as above so below'. Alan Butler and I were able to confirm this hypothesis by a variety of means, including evidence from later cultures that appear to have adopted the 366-degree principle.

The approach our Megalithic ancestors took was to divide the circle of the Earth into 366 degrees with 60 minutes per degree and 6 seconds per minute. This resulted in a second of arc on the circumference of the Earth that was 366 Megalithic Yards long. And this is, self-evidently, an amazing set of 'wheels within wheels'!

The later Minoan culture, which developed on the Mediterranean island of Crete around 2000 BC, also used the Megalithic second of arc (366 Megalithic Yards), but to them it was divided into 1,000 parts to define the Minoan 'foot' of 30.36cm.*

As Alan Butler and I have shown, any person could generate a highly accurate Megalithic Yard by measuring the movement of Venus in the evening sky using a rope, some twine, a blob of clay and a few sticks. When we first reported our findings in our book *Civilization One*, we had a completely sound theory that explained Professor Thom's findings in precise detail. A few years later we had found the proof that it was used in huge structures that predate Megalithic building by hundreds of years. We described these archaeological findings in our later book, *Before the Pyramids*.

---

* Graham, Joseph Walter, *The Palaces of Crete*, Princeton University Press, Princeton, New Jersey, 1962

## Thomas Jefferson and the ancient scientists

As I have already mentioned, Thomas Jefferson, the principal author of the Declaration of Independence and the third president of the USA, set about creating new units of measurement for his young country. Like his colleagues, statesman George Washington and prolific inventor Benjamin Franklin, Jefferson had a truly great mind. In approaching his task of creating new units of measure he started by looking at the old, chaotic units that had come from the Old World, principally England. He quickly realized that Imperial measurements were not arbitrary and not based on body parts as universally believed.

Among many original observations, Jefferson noted that it could not be coincidence that a cubic foot holds 1,000oz of rainwater – not 999 or 1001, but exactly 1,000oz. The old measures were, he concluded, all interconnected in a very deliberate but unseen way – despite the general opinion that they were a mishmash from separate sources. He noted that the measures showed that there had once been a harmonization of wet and dry measures and that all of the units he looked at were members of a group of measurement units 'from very high antiquity'.

At some point in the mists of time, Jefferson suggested, there was a deliberate plan of mathematical purity. He was clearly puzzled as to what could be behind such beauty and mathematical order: 'What circumstances of the times, or purposes of barter or commerce, called for this combination of weights and measures… a relation so integral between weights and solid measures, must have been the result of design and scientific calculation, and not a mere coincidence of hazard.'

Jefferson correctly identified that these units were due to scientists, not some dim-witted trader inventing a rough-and-ready unit to barter a length of cloth for some grain and a flagon of beer.

Jefferson was a natural scientist and a great thinker. He therefore approached his challenges with an open mind and sound reasoning. He wanted his new units to be scientifically robust, enduring and relevant to the world – so he wanted to use something natural as his starting point. It did not take him very long to realize that there is only one aspect of nature that gave rise to any reliable unit of measure – the turning of the Earth. Jefferson described how a pendulum could be used to make a linear unit from which cubes could be used to create volumetric and weight values.

## A second coming

Jefferson's methodical and logical reasoning also led him to use a pendulum to convert time into a linear unit. He decided that he should use a pendulum that had a beat of one second as the basis for his measuring system. The second of time seemed like a natural choice, as it was the universal unit of time based on a 24-hour day with 60 minutes to the hour and 60 seconds to the minute. He knew that there were therefore 86,400 seconds in a mean solar day but more importantly, 86,164 seconds in a sidereal day – one rotation of the Earth gauged by watching any star. The 236 seconds difference between the two kinds of day added up to exactly one extra day, creating the 366th day.

Jefferson explained his thinking: 'A pendulum, vibrating freely, in small and equal arcs, may be so adjusted in its length, as, by its vibrations, to make this division of the Earth's motion into 86,400 equal parts, called seconds of mean time.

'Such a pendulum, then, becomes itself a measure of determinate length, to which all others may be referred to as a standard.'

In the end, Jefferson used a 'rod' instead of a pendulum. It does exactly the same thing, but instead of being a weight on the end of a piece of string it is a ridged strip of very thin metal without a weight on the end. This means that the weight of the rod itself responds to the Earth's gravity rather than the weight at the end of a piece of twine. It is even more accurate than a pendulum, but Jefferson pointed out that such a rod will always have to be exactly 50 per cent longer than a pendulum to produce the same time interval.

Jefferson proposed a whole system of new units but they were never adopted by the USA. But taking the second of time as the basis of his rod form of pendulum caused him to link into the ancient units. This great statesman proposed a unit of length that he called a furlong, different to but named after an old British unit. He did not know it, but 366 times 366 of his newly defined furlongs was equal to the polar circumference of the Earth – as close as it is possible to measure it today: $366^2$ Jefferson furlongs = 39,961km.

The second of time was far more ancient and more special than Jefferson could ever imagine. And the metre was far from new when the French Academy thought it had invented it over 300 years ago.

## The ancient metre

The modern metre was invented by the French Academy at the same time as Jefferson was working in the USA. The Academy originally decided on its 'new' unit of length based on a simple pendulum that 'beats' at the rate of once per second, but a few years later it took this idea and adjusted it a very small amount so that it would be geodesic (fitting the Earth's circumference – in this case 1/10-millionth of the distance from the equator to the north pole).

Despite this decision, the 'seconds pendulum' was far from forgotten. It was decided that the pendulum method would be retained as a back-up to the Metre des Archives platinum bar that had been set as the standard in 1799. It was realized that war, pestilence or global disaster could conceivably cause the loss of the physical master measure and therefore a means of redefining the unit from nature must be recorded. The French commission said: 'To make observations at latitude 45° for determining the number of vibrations in a day, and in a vacuum at sea-level, of a simple pendulum equal in length when at the temperature of melting ice, to the 10-millionth part of the meridian quadrant with a view to the possibility of restoring the length of the new standard unit, at any future time, by pendulum observation.'

However, the French did not invent the metre – they merely discovered it courtesy of using a pendulum that swung at the rate of one per second between the extremities of its arc.

## The ancient metric system

We are accustomed to thinking of 60 seconds to a minute and 60 minutes to an hour because our system of time derives from that of the Sumerian and later Babylonian civilizations that occupied the area that is now Iraq and Kuwait. Prehistoric peoples known as the Ubaidians had originally settled in the region, establishing settlements that gradually developed into the important Sumerian cities of Adab, Eridu, Isin, Kish, Kullab, Lagash, Larsa, Nippur and Ur. As the region prospered, Semites from the Syrian and Arabian deserts moved in and somewhere around 3250 BC the Sumerians arrived and began to intermarry with the native population. These small, dark-haired newcomers were intellectually and technologically highly sophisticated and it is now believed that these Sumerians invented many important technologies, including glass, metalworking, writing and the wheel.

These people used a linear measure called a *kush*, which was made up of 180 *se*, and a double *kush* of 360 *se*. This is the origin of the modern 360 degrees to a circle and 360 minutes to each quarter of the day. The modern second and hour also come directly from these people.

The great Italian metrologist Professor Livio Stecchini stated that he believed the value of the double *kush* was 99.88cm and that the Sumerians used a one-tenth cube to produce it. This is what we would recognize today as a litre, and the weight of that water would be a kilogramme. All this more than 4,000 years ago.

Whilst standard archaeology is slow to admit the use of pendulums in the ancient world, it does seem contrary not to make a connection between the Sumerian second of time and their *kush* – which just happens to be the length that produces that time interval. Whilst a *kush* pendulum has a period of one second (the time it takes for the bob to swing out and return to its starting point), the double *kush* has a beat of one second (the time between each extremity of the arc).

More recently, Alan Butler and I were able to show that the second of time had been in use in England 5,500 years ago – shortly before the beginning of the great Megalithic building period. In our view there is also evidence that points strongly towards the metre (or more precisely the double *kush*) also being used at this time by henge builders. It appears that the Megalithic Yard and the second-based metre were used at the same time for inter-related purposes of astronomical observations and measurement.

Archaeologists, by and large, are not qualified, able or willing to understand and assess the finding of either Alexander Thom or the forensic work conducted by Alan Butler and myself. However, we have been able to demonstrate that prehistoric henges in Yorkshire, England, employed these 366-based units and were laid out in an unbelievably massive (and accurate) reconstruction of the stars of Orion's Belt.* Our findings regarding the presence of the EMS system and its use at prehistoric sites are based on hard evidence that has been assessed by several people highly qualified in subjects such as mathematics, physics and engineering.

It was following the publication of our book *Civilization One* that we were approached by Professor Gordon Freeman,

* Knight, C, and Butler, A, *Before the Pyramids*, Watkins, London, 2009

mentioned earlier in the chapter. He told us how he had been made aware of our work by some of some of his students who were enthusiastic about our discoveries. As mentioned, Gordon has a rare combination of talents, with doctorates in both physics and chemistry plus as an impressive background in the field of kinetics and interdisciplinary studies, as well as a deep understanding of Megalithic structures. Whilst he pointed out that our lack of training in standard methodologies had caused us to show some weaknesses in our style of technical reporting, he stated that they did not affect the accuracy of our findings and he congratulated us on making a number of major contributions to archaeology and practical geometry. He summed up by saying we were: 'Setting a new standard for archaeology and archaeoastronomy.'

## The limitations of current archaeology

Mainstream archaeologists have a view of the past world that requires the inhabitants of the British Isles to have been crude peoples with no real scientific knowledge or much in the way of social infrastructure before the Romans arrived in around AD 43. The standard approach to reconstructing the past is to use remnants of domestic life as indicators of the status of the civilization, such as fragments of ceramic pots, tools and the contents of midden heaps. Such evidence from the British Neolithic period does indeed suggest that these people were unsophisticated. But all evidence has to be considered to gain a proper view of the time.

If archaeologists 5,000 years in the future were to dig up the remains of the two adjoining villages of Collex and Bossy in Switzerland they would find fairly humble artefacts of daily life. They might find discarded wine bottles, broken lamps, a battered saucepan and the remains of some simple houses.

What they might well miss is a tunnel running more than 100m (33ft) below these villages. If they did notice it and find that it actually runs in a circle covering 27km (17 miles) they would marvel at the hard work that had gone into making the tunnel and debate its purpose. Judging by the strange theories that currently surround Stonehenge, some would argue the Swiss tunnel was a vault created for the dead. Others might put it down to worship of long-forgotten underworld deities and speculate about rituals and sacrifices.

What these archaeologists of tomorrow will not detect easily is that this was a piece of scientific equipment – one used as a particle accelerator by physicists to investigate some of the fundamental questions concerning the basic laws which govern the forces between the elementary objects, the structure of space and time, and in particular the intersection of quantum mechanics and general relativity. This circular subterranean complex is currently known as the CERN Large Hadron Collider – home to some of the brightest scientists of the 21st century.

Similar difficulties exist for archaeologists today, with the standard view of Stone Age people being that everyone lived more or less the same kind of life, hunting, fishing, farming and possibly trading goods with others. There is no expectation of an élite, a sub-group of scientists. And the failure of modern archaeologists to train their students in mathematics and statistics has blunted the possibility of even seeing such underlying patterns. This is why it took a professor of engineering to detect the Megalithic Yard and a professor of metrology to identify that the Sumerians used the metric system. Because the archaeologists are not equipped to understand such mathematically based evidence, they ignore it and continue to dream up their own, sometimes rather wacky, theories.

One leading archaeologist responded very politely to my request for him to review a brief paper on the EMS system by saying that his mathematical ability was too poor to understand this new evidence. This only serves to demonstrate that we have a current generation of academic archaeologists who are not equipped for the profession they claim to represent. As a research scientist with several decades of archaeological investigation, Gordon Freeman put it down to a generational issue, encouraging Alan Butler and me to realize it will take time for our ideas to become mainstream, saying: 'Many young archaeology students like this stuff, so patience. The best I can say for the current senior archaeologists in this field is that they will die.'

However, I completely concede that there is a massive cultural contradiction between the evidence of a crude day-to-day lifestyle and this hugely advanced scientific knowledge. The gulf is so hard to reconcile that it suggests that there was something very strange happening. Perhaps a separate group of people – possibly non-indigenous – were guiding the archaeoastronomy and the creation of units of measurement that are still in universal use today.

But there is even more behind the genius of this ancient system. Something that moves the issue from the extraordinary to the apparently impossible.

# Chapter 12

# GOD'S BLUEPRINT

'We are, by astronomical standards, a pampered,
cosseted, cherished group of creatures... If the universe
had not been made with the most exacting precision
we could never have come into existence. It is my
view that these circumstances indicate the universe
was created for man to live in.'
*John O'Keefe (astronomer at NASA)*

One big issue remains to be answered. Megalithic structures
were built across western Europe and used to observe the
movements of the Sun and the Moon, but how could the
unit of measure upon which these structures were based be
so beautifully correlated to the circumference of both these
bodies as well as of the Earth?

There seem to be three main conclusions to be made:

1. It is a coincidence that the Earth, the Moon and the Sun
   all fit the system perfectly when every other object in
   the solar system does not.

2. The Megalithic people were – 5,500 years ago – able to measure the size of the Earth, Moon and Sun and invent a system of units that worked perfectly with them all.

3. The Earth, Moon and Sun were somehow designed to integrate in this way.

Could it be a coincidence? On top of all the other strange facts regarding the Moon and its role in creating life on Earth, it becomes rather unrealistic to keep putting everything down to a random fluke of nature. Why would such multilayered, wildly improbable coincidences keep happening in the zone where we humans exist and nowhere else?

Could our Stone Age forebears really have mapped the Sun and the Moon as well as the Earth? Surely, this is not possible to believe. Archaeologists may have underestimated their scientific prowess, but to map and measure other worlds and then compute a common integer system of metrology is surely beyond modern man, let alone the inhabitants of the British Neolithic period?

The final option is conscious design. The idea of deliberate design seems unreasonable; common sense tells us it's wrong. But we must remember the wise words of Albert Einstein: 'Common sense is the collection of prejudices acquired by age eighteen.'

Experts, of whatever variety, seek to explain things in the way they were taught at university: 'If it doesn't fit my world-view it must be wrong.' But it is always good science to follow the words that Sir Arthur Conan Doyle put into the mouth of the fictional character Sherlock Holmes: 'Once you eliminate the impossible, whatever remains, no matter how improbable, must be the truth.'

It was not unreasonable to believe that the stonemasons of the Neolithic period were smart enough to measure the polar circumference of the Earth and that they devised a unit of measure that has an integer relationship to the dimensions of the planet. Such a feat can be achieved with very simple tools, as demonstrated later by the ancient Greeks. But surely they could not have measured the circumference of the Moon and the Sun?

That leaves one remaining possibility. These three bodies travelling through space are indeed the result of conscious design.

If your brain is finding it hard to be as objective as Conan Doyle suggests, then consider this: viewed from the Earth's surface the Sun is 400 times as far away as the Moon. And for some inexplicable reason the Sun is 400 times the diameter of the Moon. Bizarrely, this causes them to appear to be the same size in the sky, which is why solar eclipses occur – when the Moon passes between the Earth and the Sun, they fit like two overlapping coins.

But there is more: the amount of sky that the Sun and the Moon take up is half a Megalithic degree (a degree being 1/366th part of the heavens). That is a very human aspect because this visual equilibrium only occurs when viewed from our standpoint on the surface of the Earth at this point in our planet's history.

The value 366 keeps on repeating. It a physical fact that the Earth's circumference is 366 per cent greater than that of the Moon. (Does anyone still want to argue for a coincidence?)

Conversely, the Moon's circumference is 27.322 per cent that of the Earth, which doesn't sound too meaningful – except that the Moon turns once on its axis and orbits the Earth once every 27.322 Earth days! By what strange mechanism do the relative circumferences of the Earth and its Moon conspire to be the same value as its orbital period measured in Earth days?

The relative sizes of these bodies and time measured in days are completely unrelated. It is not the result of any mechanism – it seems like it is a deliberate echo to draw attention to these values.

As the table shows, it is the repeating values that make the Earth, Moon and Sun relationship so special. And there is a direct connection with the speed of light. For all the world, it is as though someone designed the set-up with the detailed perfection of the proverbial Swiss clock.

There are three numbers, together with their divisions and multiples, that keep on repeating for the Earth, Moon and Sun. These numbers are 366, 27.322 and 100.

Another strangeness of the Moon is the way that it imitates the apparent position of the Sun when viewed by people on the planet's surface.

The point on the horizon at which the Sun rises or sets marks the point at which the Moon will appear six months apart. There is no astronomical explanation for this miracle of observational astronomy. It does not happen for any reason of necessary planetary mechanics – other than it was planned that way.

The henges (circular or near-circular structures) of prehistoric Britain were divided using 732 poles (366 × 2). Because the Sun and the Moon each occupy half of a Megalithic degree

| 366 | There are 366 rotations or 'star days' in an Earth year. |
|---|---|
| | The rising/setting Sun and Moon have a combined width of one 366th part of the horizon. |
| | There are 366 degrees in a circle according to Megalithic geometry. |
| | There are 366 Megalithic Yards to one Megalithic second of arc of the polar circumference of the Earth. |
| | The circumference of the Earth is 366 per cent larger than the Moon. |
| | 366 lunar orbits of the Earth take 10,000 days. |
| **27.322** | The circumference of the Moon is 27.322 per cent that of the Earth. |
| | The rotational period of the Moon is the same as its orbital period – 27.322 days. |
| **100, 400, 10,000 and 40,000** | There are 100 Megalithic Yards to one lunar degree. |
| | The Moon's orbital speed is 100 times slower than the Earth's. |
| | The Moon's circumference is 400 times smaller than that of the Sun. |
| | The Moon is 400 times closer to the Earth than the Sun. |
| | There are 40,000 Megalithic Yards to one solar degree. |
| | There are 40,000km to the Earth's polar circumference. |
| | The Earth orbits the Sun at 1/10,000th the speed of light. |
| | In 10,000 days the Moon completes 366 turns on its axis. |

of the horizon, each would fit exactly when viewed from the centre of the henge.

Science is the process of noting observable facts very carefully and then using them to draw conclusions about the way things work. It is not up to anyone to put restrictions on what those conclusions might be – the truth will speak for itself. If one keeps an open mind, it would appear that the number patterning in everything to do with the Earth has been planned. The only reasonable explanations are that aliens set up everything or God created heaven and Earth for our benefit.

If it was aliens who seeded the Earth from the start, then they did this more than 4.5 billion years ago – that is 4,500,000,000 years in the past. To have had such super-advanced abilities back then they must have evolved very early in the development of the universe. Assuming that they have survived the dangers of the cosmos, since that time they would have effectively evolved to become as perfect as God. Imagine how far humans will have evolved in the future over such a massive period. The time frame involved is 20 times greater than that covered since our forebears were small hamster-like creatures.

However, it is extremely unlikely that any life form could have evolved to such an advanced level so early in the development of the universe. That means the likelihood of God as the power behind the creation of the Earth seems irresistible. Even an open-minded atheist will have to admit that the possibility has now to be taken very seriously.

One assumption about God is that He has boundless powers – and any intellect that can balance the rules of physics so perfectly in favour of life has to be omnipotent.

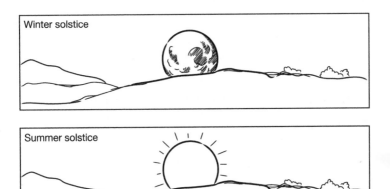

The Sun and the Moon appear to be same size in the sky because the Moon is 1/400th of the Sun's size but is, amazingly, 400 times closer to the Earth. Each of these heavenly bodies covers half of a Megalithic degree of the arc of the sky. If they could be viewed side by side they would mark a very neat 1 megalithic degree.

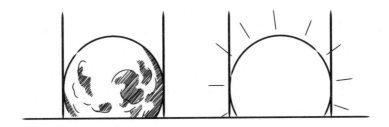

The question then is, why does He need humans, and, if He does, why does He not create them without imperfections and why does He not talk directly to them?

The answers to such questions are firmly in the realms of theological philosophy. Great minds have considered such questions since history began. Many believe that freewill has to exist and that God's whole purpose is to create creatures that make their own judgements. Whatever the reason, it seems that there is some communication directed from the creator towards us today.

## Base ten communications

It appears that our planet and its Moon were built using ratios and units that relate to the Sun, and are so remarkable that they would, once found out, cause any intelligent life form to pay attention.

If the Earth was created, along with the Sun and the Moon – who planned them? What sort of a 'God' might have been responsible for our existence? How far did the intervention of this potential creator extend? Was it simply a matter of supplying the Earth with a suitable Moon, in order to ensure the sort of stability that would ultimately lead to advanced life, or was a much more tangible and personal relationship intended? How much did this creative force, no matter what form it might have taken, know about the ultimate result of the exercise? Was it aware that the intelligent species that finally lifted its head from the savannah to stare at the starry vaults of heaven would be a ten-fingered, ten-toed bipedal anthropoid?

## How special is the Earth?

If the Earth, Moon and Sun were created to produce intelligent life, how come our solar system is just a tiny dot in the vast expanse of the cosmos?

A new theory that has gained a lot of credence suggests that we might not be as unimportant as generally assumed since the early part of the 20th century.

For most of human history there has been a rather egotistic idea that we humans are entirely central to God's creation. Everything was believed to have been made for our benefit. But ever since Nicolaus Copernicus suggested that the Earth was just one of many planets in a system with the Sun at its centre, the idea that we are just a dot in an infinite universe grew to become the most widely held view of science and most non-religious laypeople.

The Copernican, or cosmological, principle, as it is known, states that nothing distinguishes the position of Earth or our galaxy from any other place in the entire universe. But could this modern idea be wrong?

The Copernican principle today is based on two ideas: that the universe is both homogeneous and isotropic. Homogeneous means that whilst there may be localized differences, averaged over large enough scales the universe has the same properties everywhere. Isotropic means that the universe appears to have the same properties when viewed in any direction from every location; basically, the idea is that if you could plant your feet firmly on any alien planet at any point in the cosmos, the sky would look pretty similar to what we see from here, in every direction, which means that there is no centre and no outer fringe to the universe.

This principle was totally embedded in the cosmological establishment until 1998, when astronomers studying stellar explosions known as type 1a supernovae made a discovery that raised eyebrows around the world. It was accepted wisdom that supernovae are uniformly bright and therefore the fainter they appear the more distant they must be. But the furthest supernovae were so faint that they would have to be an impossible distance away. This suggested that at some time over the last 2 or 3 billion years they must have begun to accelerate away from us. Rather than the universe's expansion slowing down as expected, it seemed as though it has been speeding up.

This problem was solved by inventing a hypothetical substance called 'dark energy'. This undetectable energy was thought to pervade space, overwhelming the force of gravity and driving the accelerating expansion. No one really knows what it is, where it comes from or even if it exists at all, but it was accepted that this dark energy would have to account for around 73 per cent of the total mass-energy of the entire universe to be responsible for what we see.

Space exploration is now beginning to give us a better understanding of this makeup of the universe. The Wilkinson Microwave Anisotropy Probe (WMAP) is a NASA Explorer mission that launched in June 2001 to make fundamental measurements of the properties of our universe as a whole. WMAP is considered to have been stunningly successful, completing a new Standard Model of Cosmology in January 2013.

By making accurate measurements of the cosmic microwave background fluctuations, WMAP was able to measure the composition of the universe to an accuracy of better than a few per cent of the overall density. The breakdown shows that 4.6 per cent is atoms (solid matter). More than 95 per cent of the energy density in the universe is in a form that has never been directly detected in the laboratory: 24 per cent is cold dark matter and 71.4 per cent is dark energy.

If 71.4 per cent of the energy density in the universe is in the form of dark energy, which has a gravitationally repulsive effect, it is just the right amount to explain both the flatness of the universe and the observed accelerated expansion. Whilst no one knows what this dark energy actually is, its observable properties are assumed to define its existence.

There is also an opinion expressed by George Ellis, a leading cosmology theorist at the University of Cape Town, who is focused on the philosophy of cosmology in that he takes the view that we need to think beyond describing what we consider to be the physical. He has raised an important suggestion: 'If we analyse the supernova data by assuming the Copernican principle is correct and get out something unphysical, I think we should start questioning the Copernican principle.'

According to Ellis and other cosmologists, our uncertainty about galaxy distances could mean that the distribution of matter looks the same in all directions – and yet varies with distance from us. This suggests that the Earth might be sitting right in the middle of a 'void', an unbelievably vast spherical bubble in an otherwise homogeneous universe. This giant bubble contains the billions of stars and galaxies we see from Earth, but beyond that, where everything is too far away for us to see, the stars and galaxies are far more densely packed together.

159

This new theory leads to an even more astonishing conclusion. For things such as the cosmic background radiation to appear isotropic to us from within this void, our little planet would have to be at the centre of the entire visible universe!

This theory makes great sense of all the available evidence. Techniques to investigate this amazing possibility are being developed right now. But if the Earth is at the centre of all we see out in space, surely that makes us humans entirely special? Perhaps we are the whole reason for the visible universe existing at all? This seems like a theological idea, but it is entirely scientifically based.

Did the creator God build everything we see through our finest telescopes as a way to prepare the cosmos for human beings?

## Is there a message?

This could be the logical next question: Is there a message from the creator of the universe addressed to the modern world?

Whoever or whatever God is, He does not appear to have had any direct contact for a long time – except, of course, in the hearts of some religious believers. The scriptures of most religions have been frozen in time for millennia. There were many prophets who supposedly spoke with God in Judaism, Christianity and Islam, but only two leaders of religion have interfaced directly with God since the prophet Muhammad died in Medina on 8 June 632. Both of those leaders are relatively recent: Sayyid 'Ali Muhammad Shirazi, the Bab

(1819–50), and his successor Mirza Husayn 'Ali Nuri Baha' Allah (1817–92). They left behind many volumes of supposed scriptures, all of which are deemed by their followers to be nothing less than the direct word of God.

According to Christian tradition, God made a brief personal appearance as a man travelling around a small patch of desert in the Middle East some 2,000 years ago. Born Yeshua, a Jewish teacher from a priestly bloodline, he is worshipped today under the Greek designation Jesus Christ and assigned the status of the 'Son of God' and the Jewish Messiah.

Those ancient otherworldly contacts by God were conducted in the style of their times: men with flowing beards standing on mountains holding tablets of stone bearing God's words. Today, we might expect contact from the creator to take a different form.

Around 50 years ago, at a time when space research was all the rage and the USA and the USSR were vying to be the first nation to land men on the Moon, a brand new organization came into existence. SETI, which stands for Search for Extra Terrestrial Intelligence, was the brainchild of an electrical engineer, who naturally focused his attention on radio astronomy. The man in question was Frank Drake, and what he wanted to know was whether someone, or something, out there in the depths of space might be trying to talk to us via radio waves.

Drake and others reasoned that in a universe that is filled with quite naturally occurring radio signals, there might be one or even several messages that had been generated intentionally – saying something as simple as 'Hi there. We are here'. SETI originally had financial support from NASA, although it is now an independent organization. The whole idea captured the public imagination at the time and to some extent it still does. Millions of people throughout the world devote a chunk of their personal computer 'down time' to help SETI wade through the morass of radio waves that bombard the Earth every day, trying to work out if any of them might have been created intentionally. But what are they listening for? What sort of message would alien life forms choose to create on the off-chance that some other sentient living creatures might be listening in a time frame that could result in a response?

Drake's work had a huge cultural impact, generating a fascination with alien life that helped to spark TV series such as *Star Trek*, and films such as *2001: A Space Odyssey*, as well as countless sci-fi books.

It seems logical to assume that the laws of physics are something to which all sentient life forms would inevitably turn their attention. After all, any species that could either send or receive radio broadcasts of any kind would have to understand the basic laws of physics, and as a result SETI assumes that what we would be most likely to receive would be a mathematical pattern – for example, something relating to prime numbers, to pi, phi or to other number sequences, or mathematical equations that would stand out from the background of naturally occurring radio signals.

Radio emissions from space are perfectly natural in origin – they occur right across the electromagnetic spectrum – and because SETI could not listen to all of them, some decision had to be made as to the possible frequency an extraterrestrial transmitter might choose to use. In 1959 two young scientists from Cornell University in the USA addressed this problem in an article for *Nature* magazine. Phillip Morrison and Giuseppe Cocconi came to the conclusion that the best place to look for an intended signal would be in the 1420MHz range, since they reasoned that this was a fairly 'quiet' part of the spectrum and therefore one that a prospective communicator was likely to choose. SETI followed the pair's advice and this is the frequency range that is still being monitored on a daily basis.

Whilst SETI has good intentions, from a statistical viewpoint what is the chance that we will actually 'hear' any message that has been sent, even assuming such a communication has ever existed? Frank Drake came up with what became known as the Drake equation. The conclusion was that there may well be thousands of intergalactic civilizations, and that any of them could be broadcasting messages into space, hoping to contact other life forms. Even if this is true, the chances of us latching onto such a signal are extraordinarily poor. SETI has now been tuned into space for a matter of only 50 years or so, whereas the Earth has existed for around 4.6 billion years. Humanity itself, in the form of *Homo sapiens*, has been present for around 200,000 years, though only capable of hearing any sort of radio broadcast for a century or so.

And, should we survive for a few more centuries, it may well be that radio signals are about as important to our lives as smoke signals or the pigeon post!

Even assuming there was an intelligent species out there somewhere that was trying to get in touch with their neighbours in space, they would have had to reach a period of technological expertise at the same time as us, or at least at a period commensurate with the fantastic distances involved in space. Bearing in mind that nothing in space is supposed to travel faster than the speed of light, and also recognizing that stars and galaxies exist at a vast distance from us, any proposed message that does reach us could have been travelling for thousands or millions of years. And if we should ever receive such an intended message, the culture that sent it may well have ceased to exist during the long intervening period, or else tired of sending messages of any sort. Supposing this is not the case, it would take an equally protracted period for our reply to get back to the source of the original message. All things considered, it doesn't look good for intergalactic telephone calls.

Some astronomers are now beginning to rethink all their assumptions about the likelihood of ever finding alien life. Howard Smith, a senior astrophysicist at Harvard University, said in January 2011: 'The new information we are getting suggests we could effectively be alone in the universe. There are very few solar systems or planets like ours... It means it is highly unlikely there are any planets with intelligent life close enough for us to make contact.'

Smith believes that the time has come to rewrite the famous Drake equation and bin its estimate of the likelihood of contacting alien life. When the formula was introduced, back in 1961, it multiplied factors such as the rate of star formation, the proportion of stars likely to have planets and the fraction that might develop intelligent life to suggest that there were likely to be around 10 detectable advanced civilizations in the Milky Way. The assumption was used to justify the creation of SETI, which today employs 150 scientists and other staff in the search for alien contact. But Smith's 2011 paper, delivered at the annual meeting of the American Association for the

Advancement of Science, argued that the optimistic estimates put into the Drake equation have generated a grossly inflated value for the chances of finding alien intelligence.

## Rethinking the medium of a message

Back in August 2004 an article appeared in the magazine *New Scientist*, authored by Paul Davies, then a scientist at the Australian Centre for Astrobiology at Macquarie University (subsequently relocated to UNSW – University of New South Wales) in Sydney. Davies complimented SETI for its tireless efforts across four decades, but wondered whether radio signals are a reliable way of passing a message to another species, bearing in mind the timescale and distances involved. Wouldn't it be more likely, Davies suggested, that any such species, which may be immeasurably older than our own, would leave us a more enduring message than a fairly random and easily overlooked radio signal?

Davies suggested that instead of radio transmissions any advanced creatures elsewhere in the galaxy or beyond would be more likely to have chosen to leave 'artefacts' in the vicinity of worlds that looked as though they might one day give rise to intelligent life – something that any such future species could not fail to recognize.

Meanwhile, Professor Christopher Rose, of Rutgers University in New Jersey, and Gregory Wright, a physicist with Antiope Associates, also in New Jersey, are on record as saying that the transmission by an extraterrestrial civilization of a radio signal, which may well have to be detected 10,000 light years away, does not make any sense. They also believe that it would be far more efficient to send us some kind of message inscribed on physical matter – a kind of 'message in a bottle'. And they believe such a message could already be waiting for us in our own backyard. We merely have to find it, and to recognize it as a clear message.

Professor Rose observed that, when considering any sort of intergalactic communication, 'if energy is what you care about, it's tremendously more efficient to toss a rock'. Once radio signals pass us by they are gone forever, so aliens would have to beam signals continuously over millions of years. And since we have only had radio for a minuscule fraction of our existence as an advanced species it is quite likely that such signals could well have been missed.

Given that the Earth is in a constant state of flux, with mountains rising and falling, continents shifting and seas roaming the planet's surface, the question arises as to what medium could sustain a message for millions or even billions of years? Well, the only place that has remained entirely stable is the Moon.

## Is the Moon a message?

Could the Moon itself be a message? Once the ancient EMS system is applied to it, it shines out like a neon light on a wet and foggy night.

If there is a message being delivered to us in the shape of the relationship of the Earth, Moon and Sun there is no reason to attribute it to aliens because there is no reason whatsoever to suppose that aliens exist. But a creator God is thought to be entirely possible by the majority of scientists.

There are lots of reasons to suspect that such an entity did, and no doubt still does, exist.

If God did make life on Earth possible by His organization of the laws of physics and the structure of the Earth and Moon, did He leave it at that or did He create a message that we could understand, when we were ready?

To say that the Moon and its relationship with the Earth and the Sun is odd is a total understatement. And it is strange in the extreme that our Megalithic ancestors appear to have known about the underlying relationships and units of measure that arise from these relationships.

First of all there is the presence of solar eclipses – those times when the disc of the Moon fits neatly and absolutely across the disc of the Sun. If ever there was a message that said 'Look! Take Notice!' this is surely represented by the total darkening of the sky during the middle of the day. Total eclipses scared the hell out of our ancestors, and the astronomers of many ancient civilizations went to incredible lengths to predict them. By the laws of chance the possibility of such a happening is very, very remote. It works because the Moon is 1/400th part of the size of the Sun and because it is capable of standing 1/400th part of the distance between the Earth and the Sun. The coincidence is deepened by that very round, decimal '400'. After all, even if such an outrageous happening as a solar eclipse did take place, the number involved could not have been any other.

Total eclipses of the sort we see today, and have seen throughout human history, did not always happen. In the distant past things were very different and they will not occur in the distant future. This is because the Moon's orbit is expanding over time as it slows down. A 'mere' billion years ago, the Moon was around twice as large in the sky as it is today, and it took only 20 days to orbit the Earth. Also, one Earth 'day' was about 18 hours long, so none of the beauty of the EMS system existed.

The Moon is gradually receding from the Earth into a higher orbit, and it has been calculated that this will continue for about 50 billion years and then the Earth and Moon will be trapped in a 'spin–orbit resonance'. At this point the Moon and Earth would rotate around their axes in the same time, always facing each other with the same side. At this time the Moon will be a mere speck in the night sky, lost among the background stars.

It follows that any message in the structure of the Earth–Moon–Sun relationship is time critical. It works now – in the human period of our planet's lifecycle. With our present level of intelligence and our understanding of the laws of probability these patterns should be alerting us instantly to the fact that there is something very strange taking place in our own backyard.

If any such series of mathematical peculiarities were to be received by the scientists at SETI, news broadcasts all over the planet would be filled with shouts of 'We have found evidence that there is intelligent life out there in space'. It is precisely the sort of message SETI is looking for and it exists in our own immediate environment. There is only one reasonable conclusion to be drawn: this is all part of a 'set and forget' system, the originator of which somehow knew how things would pan out with the passing of 4.6 billion years and that there would be people around with ten fingers who would be in a position, in terms of intelligence, to recognize what had taken place.

Ten fingers are important because this has caused humans to choose base ten as the standard means of counting. For example, it is conspicuous that the Moon completes 366 lunar orbits of the Earth in a neat 10,000 days – but it would seem very different if we had four fingers, or six fingers on each hand.

|  | Lunar orbits | Days |
|---|---|---|
| Five fingers per hand (Base ten) | 366 | 10,000 |
| Four fingers per hand (Base eight) | 556 | 23,420 |
| Six fingers per hand (Base twelve) | 266 | 5,954 |

If all of the many Earth, Moon and Sun relationships illuminated by the EMS system are a blueprint, they refer to the finished product rather than to the point of creation. By finished product, I mean right now – the point at which human kind has reached some level of scientific and cultural maturity.

If God did create us for some greater purpose, we must surely be ripe – ready for direct communication from our maker. In a little more than a century and a half, the world has changed from a network of isolated communities – with no external communication for the masses, and only horses as the primary means of transport and the posted letter as the main means of communication over distance for the well-to-do – to an interconnected global village. People now routinely fly around our planet and even remote villages have television, email and the Internet to connect them to the entire world and stream them information. We are now, arguably, ready and able to understand a communication from God – in the language of 21st-century science rather than folklore and superstition.

The problem is that although we are largely intellectually mature, we also now have the means to destroy ourselves. The so-called Cold War between the West and the Soviet Union during the second half of the 20th century was only prevented from turning into the real thing thanks to the concept of Mutually Assured Destruction (MAD) – the fact that both sides had nuclear weapons created a standoff. But now, just a few years later, we are in a position where less rational states are close to having the ability to deliver death on a gigantic scale. Some are driven by a godless pursuit of totalitarian dictatorship and others by a belief that their religious scriptures demand the destruction of everyone who does not worship God in their preferred way.

If there ever was a time when we need a communication from the intellect that planned the whole of creation – this is it. We need to have the next level of guidance, conceivably in an entirely explicit manner.

So, if the Moon is our wake-up call, what is the message?

The very size of the Moon may be part of a clue. The circumference of the Earth is 366 per cent greater than that of the Moon. And we can look at the same facts in a different way. The size of the Moon is 27.322 per cent that of the Earth, and of course 27.322 days is the number of days in the orbit of the Moon. This simply should not happen and it is not 'numerology' or random 'number plucking'. These number relationships are very real and they occur time and again.

The reason we should quite definitely take notice is that we are dealing with related but different aspects of the Earth–Moon–Sun relationships and yet the numbers come out to the same each time. On the one hand we are dealing with the physical size of the bodies concerned and on the other we are talking about their orbital characteristics. These are not related and any relationship between them has changed across time. It is only now, at this particular point in the Earth's development, that that they show these amazing correspondences.

Any one of these peculiarities might be put down to a strange coincidence. What is not half as easy to explain is why they appear so frequently and are all related numerically to each other. They are all variations on the same theme and they all rely in part on the size and orbital characteristics of the Earth, the Moon and the Sun. They all turn irrational numbers into a rational number: $27.322 \times 366 = 10,000$

If that is not shouting 'pay attention', I really can't think what it would take to wake us up!

Scientists such as Paul Davies have said that we should be looking for a message of the 'set and forget' type. A medium that is either very big and robust, in order to endure for billions of years, or very small and in massive numbers so that some will survive through all kinds of catastrophe. But it could be both – the extremely large working together with the invisibly small to deliver a message of vital importance.

## A living message

When it comes to the very large, the Moon fits the bill like nothing else could. Huge and unchanging across billions of years, it is visible to everyone on the planet on most days. It is the ultimate noticeboard.

So what in our environment could provide the other half of a potential message? The requirements are that this medium is:

- Small and robust enough to survive all varieties of disaster
- Has been around unchanged for several billions of years
- Can be found in every part of the planet
- Is known to contain a massive amount of information.

At first this question might seem to have no answer. The requirements sound impossible – but they are not.

What then could possibly fulfil all of these criteria? When Alan Butler and I began the search for something in nature that could provide humans with a reproducible and exact measure – it actually took us just a matter of days to realize there was only one solution. And that was the turning of the Earth on its axis. Nothing else works.

So, too, the question of what could be the safe repository of super-ancient knowledge. One answer lies inside every sinew of our bodies, every fibre of every leaf, of every plant and the slime trail of every snail. The answer is deoxyribonucleic acid – DNA, the instruction manual for all life.

Things don't get much smaller than DNA. Most people are aware that DNA is the code of life itself. It exists in all living cells and contains the information necessary to create everything, from an amoeba to a blue whale. All the hereditary information that replicates any life form is held in the long strings of DNA, which even for the most basic of creatures is a fantastically complicated structure.

Inside cells, DNA exists as long chemical structures, which are called chromosomes. These chromosomes duplicate before a cell divides to create a copy. The whole business is incredibly sophisticated and yet even the very earliest creatures that inhabited the Earth already had DNA, or its companion RNA in the case of viruses, otherwise they could not have replicated.

The very existence of DNA has led many people to speculate that the presence of this most marvellous of molecules is, in itself, proof positive of the existence of God. The writer and researcher Lyall Watson suggested in his book *Supernature* that the odds against such a complex mechanism as DNA occurring by chance were greater than the known number of atoms in the universe.

The late Professor Sir Fred Hoyle, a well-respected member of the scientific community, once said: 'Rather than accept the fantastically small probability of life having arisen through the blind forces of nature, it seemed better to suppose that the origin of life was a deliberate intellectual act. By "better" I mean less likely to be wrong.'

Meanwhile, Peter T. Mora of the Macromolecular Biology Section, Immunology Program, National Cancer Institute in Bethesda, Maryland, USA, wrote: 'The presence of a living unit is exactly opposite to what we would expect on the basis of pure statistical and probability considerations.'

One influential figure, who eventually came to believe that DNA in particular may well point at an intelligence underpinning life, was Professor Anthony Flew. As discussed earlier in this book, Flew was a dyed-in-the-wool atheist until it became clear to him that the evidence amassed by science clearly demonstrated to his sceptical mind that intelligence must have been involved in the creation of DNA.

How could it be that random bits of matter could come together and create something as elegant and complex as

DNA? In 2004, astrobiologist Paul Davies observed: 'Most people take the existence of life for granted, but to a physicist like me it seems astounding. How do stupid atoms do such clever things? Physicists normally think of matter in terms of inert, clod-like particles jostling each other, so the elaborate organisation of the living cell appears little short of miraculous. Evidently, living organisms represent a state of matter in a class apart from the rest.'

It used to be thought, and still is in many scientific circles, that life developed in the chemical 'soup' that existed on the early Earth. Numerous attempts have been made to replicate what is supposed to have happened quite naturally. The first took place in the 1950s, when a graduate student from Chicago University created the exact conditions that were present in the primordial oceans of the Earth. By collecting the right chemicals together and then subjecting the mixture to synthetic lightning bolts, Miller was delighted to discover that he had created amino acids, which are the chemicals necessary for DNA and for life. Unfortunately, that is all he managed to create and to this day, despite repeated claims to the contrary, no scientist has actually created even a single-celled creature. We can read complex genomes, replace parts of cells with material from other cells and even clone animals, but up to the time of us writing this book nobody has created life. And as far as DNA is concerned, a fundamental mystery still remains: how DNA came about in the first place, because from what we understand to date, only DNA can create DNA.

No aspect of biology has received more attention in the recent past than DNA, which has been studied in minute detail in laboratories all over the world. One of the puzzles that has come to intrigue researchers over the years is why so much of the information within strings of DNA appears to do absolutely nothing. Huge amounts of information that have no apparent purpose whatsoever.

Physicist, cosmologist and astrobiologist Paul Davies has been as fascinated as we are by humanity's attempts to contact other sentient species out there in space, but like us he is somewhat sceptical regarding the possible success of organizations such as SETI, for all the reasons outlined earlier. Nevertheless, Professor Davies does not rule out the chance of a contact occurring. He has suggested: 'But what if the truth isn't out there at all? What if it lies somewhere else? Now may be the time to try a radically different approach.'

Davies is also a supporter of the 'set and forget' message, proposing: '… a legion of small, cheap, self-repairing and self-replicating machines that can keep editing and copying information and perpetuate themselves over immense durations in the face of unforeseen environmental hazards'.

And then he went on to say: 'Fortunately, such machines already exist. They are called living cells.' Davies speculated that any message placed inside living cells – specifically within DNA – could last as long as life on Earth itself. We could, in effect, each be walking telegrams, though up to now we haven't managed to read the message, or even to realize that it is present within us all.

A potential problem here might be that as life replicates, it also gradually mutates and Professor Davies pointed out that this might turn the original message into nonsense – were it not for one important fact: there are large sections of the DNA genome that appear to do nothing at all. These sections are generally labelled 'junk DNA' – apparently useless lumps of data that are more or less totally immune to degradation, even across vast periods of time.

The idea that DNA contains a message is one shared by more and more scientists.

When a team of genomic researchers at the Lawrence Berkeley National Laboratory in California presented their own findings in June 2004 the audience gasped in unison. Those listening simply could not believe what they were hearing from Edward Rubin and his team, who were reporting that they had destroyed huge sections of the genome of mice without it making any discernable difference to the animals under test. The result was truly amazing because the deleted sequences included what is known as 'conserved regions', which were previously assumed to have been protected because they contained vital information about functions. One of the sections removed by Rubin and his team was 1.6 million DNA bases long and another was 800,000 bases long, and yet the mice offspring grew and thrived as if nothing had happened.

It remains a fact that the redundant DNA sequences are as well protected as any other, which means that whatever information they contain has remained the same for billions of years. Paul Davies saw this as an ideal place to plant a message, or perhaps a whole series of messages, in the knowledge that it would stay intact for eons and even indefinitely. Elaborating on this possibility, he said: 'Looking for messages in living cells has the virtue that DNA is being sequenced anyway. All it needs is a computer to search for suspicious-looking patterns. Long strings of the same nucleotides are an obvious attention-grabber. Peculiar numerical sequences like prime numbers would be a clincher and patterns that stand out even when partially degraded by mutational noise would make the most sense… if a sequence of junk DNA bases were displayed as an array of pixels on a screen (with the colour depending on the base: blue for A, green for G, and so on), and a simple image like a ragged circle resulted, the presumption of tampering would be inescapable.'

The available space within the DNA sequence could easily accommodate a wealth of information and, unlike a random radio message, it would remain present until the day someone decided to find out what it might say.

It seems strange that this information is coming to light at exactly the same time as we are beginning to realize just how peculiar our solar system, and in particular the Moon, truly is. But perhaps it isn't strange at all, and it could well be that the 'intention' of whomever or whatever arranged things so carefully for us was, from the start, that there would come a time when we would be emotionally and intellectually ready to get a long and precise 'letter from God'.

So, potentially, we have the sort of messages that many commentators are suggesting would be most likely: something very big and something extremely small – a twin approach that seems both sensible and logical.

## Putting a message into DNA

If there was a message from the beginning of life on Earth 3.5 billion years ago, there could be no receptacle for it other than DNA. Everything else has been destroyed by the ravages of time and tide, meteor bombardment and the natural degradation of mountains, deserts, oceans and even continents. The only hiding place was in the cells of every speck of life clinging on to survival for the sake of a bigger, better, evolved future. As long as one species of something survived – the message would remain intact.

Those who deny evolution (usually on the basis of their unsophisticated analysis of ancient scriptures) surely deny God. God gave us eyes and brains and the power to reason – so why throw reason out of the window just because some low-rent religious teacher told you to? Do the reported words of Gautama Buddha, Yahweh, Jesus or the prophet Muhammad really represent what they meant to communicate? From my own limited researches into ancient Judaism and early Christianity, I suspect a lot of the original message has been lost through time and translation.

Surely life on Earth is a journey – a pathway from zero to somewhere special. We humans have a responsibility to play our part in our planet's development. We are, to the best of our species' knowledge, the highest form of intelligence anywhere – absolutely anywhere across all of time and space.

The process of inbuilt experimentation and improvement cannot be an accident of a crazed universe. Just as the starting rules of creation were unmistakably planned to produce life, so life itself appears to have been fixed to carry a substantial message.

But how do we know that DNA can be created so that it can carry a message above and beyond the coding that produces another frog, zebra or human? At the forefront of recent research is a genetic entrepreneur by the name of Craig Venter. His team of researchers have already created a new life form.

Scientists at the J. Craig Venter Institute in Rockville, Maryland, USA, stitched together every 'letter' of a genetic code in their laboratory to form an artificial chromosome 1 million characters long. The organism they shaped was very humble – a variation of a bacterium that causes mastitis in goats. In truth it was not the creation of life but an impressive construction of a new entity from existing building blocks.

Venter is a smart man but he is not playing God, as some people have suggested. Not by a long way.

However, Venter and his team decided to go beyond the manual for self-replication and add to the 'invented' creature some information that was not directly necessary, in order to ensure that the genome would always be identifiable as synthetic – they spliced fresh strands of DNA into the code to provide a biological 'watermark' that would do nothing for the final organism except carry coded messages.

One of those 'watermark' messages hidden in the code was a line from the celebrated Irish author James Joyce: 'To live, to err, to fall, to triumph, to recreate life out of life.'

James Joyce died in 1941 and his much-admired words might survive for 100 or even 1,000 years or more before the civilization that appreciates his prose finally ends. But as part of the Earth's pool of DNA his genius might endure for a billion – even a trillion – years. There is no greater immortality than that which comes with the certainty of being passed on from generation to generation. An enviable message in a world where death and degradation are otherwise guaranteed.

Venter's efforts are admirable but probably unimportant in the grand scheme of real life. Unimportant other than that they demonstrate that messages can reside in DNA – the basic coding of life. Immutable and unchanging.

However, science is moving fast.

In mid 2012 it was reported that George Church, a bioengineer, and Sri Kosuri, a geneticist, at Harvard's Wyss Institute, had successfully stored an astonishing 5.5 petabits of data (that's around 700 terabytes – or 14,000 large Blu-ray discs) in just one gram of DNA, smashing the previous DNA data density record a thousandfold. DNA was being treated as a biological digital storage device.

DNA has been identified as a potential storage medium for three reasons: it can store one bit per base (and a base is only a few atoms in size); it's volumetric; and it's incredibly stable – DNA can survive for hundreds of thousands of years without any special conditions.

The study of DNA has grown rapidly. Whilst it took years for the original Human Genome Project to analyse a single human genome of around 3 billion DNA base pairs, modern microfluidic chips can do it in hours. Scientists now foresee a world where biological storage would allow us to record anything and everything without limit. The bottom line is that DNA is like an invention from a distant science fiction future, where the impossible has become possible. But the odd point is that DNA is the most ancient 'machine' imaginable, being billions of years old.

# Chapter 13

# WHAT NEXT?

'In this bright future you can't forget your past.'
*Bob Marley*

Because of accidental discoveries I made about the Moon, which arose from my studies in Megalithic metrology, I have come to the conclusion that there is an intelligence underpinning our very existence. There was some massive intellect behind the creation of the Earth as an incubator for life.

The Moon is simply too big, too light in mass for its size, too specific in its dimensions and too useful for its existence to have been a random chance event. It reflects absolutely accurately a measuring system that must have been designed with the dimensions of the Earth in mind in that it turns every 366 Megalithic Yards of the Earth's geometry into the 100 Megalithic Yards of its own.

Nobody now disputes that without the Moon the Earth would have continued to spin wildly, may often have toppled over because of its peculiar internal structure, and would not have maintained a very specific angle relative to the Sun that would allow even warming and cooling and therefore enabling liquid water to exist on its surface.

The Moon has been our saviour in every sense of the word and has continued to perform its obviously pre-programmed tasks across virtually the whole history of the Earth. It would be absurd to suggest that so many factors as we have identified could have come together by mere chance, and faced with a mountain of apparent coincidences, the 'accidentally-out-of-chaos' theory of life begins to look totally absurd. It is not an explanation but rather an excuse for us 'not' having a sensible explanation.

The numbers 19, 27.322, 366 and 400, together with their multiples and subdivisions, crop up many times in terms of Earth, Moon and Sun relationships, and as if to make certain that we would one day 'look' at these peculiarities, we have a Moon of exactly the right size and occupying the right orbit to create regular and extremely accurate and spectacular eclipses of the Sun.

Thanks in the main to the specifics of the Earth's turning about its own axis and its path around the Sun, modern man has developed a measuring system (which, as we have seen, is not modern at all) that has properties one could never expect of a randomly chosen system.

Meanwhile, we live on a planet that has an orbital velocity of an astonishingly beautiful 1/10,000th part of the speed of light, set into a solar system that appears to have been custom-designed to protect the Earth from incoming debris, thus allowing long periods of stable conditions during which life has evolved and developed.

Despite our best endeavours we humans are as far away as ever from creating life ourselves, even though we know so much about it and have advanced techniques and all the necessary chemical constituents at our fingertips. And it may well be that within the very heart of life, inside the DNA of our own bodies, there could be a message waiting to tell us where we came from and who started the whole process.

It is not currently possible to understand or even speculate about the nature of the creative force that was apparently present in the dimensionless void that existed some 4.6 billion years ago. What kind of consciousness could arrange the laws of physics and the structure of our solar system and then create evolving life?

But if we humans choose to look at the evidence in front of us – as Megalithic man apparently did just before the dawn of history – we might enter a new phase of development. If we do, it is possible that we will have our answer very quickly indeed.

Arguably, there has never been a time in human history when we have needed more to reconnect with our maker. Millions of people believe that written scriptures from thousands of years ago provide everything we need to know about God. But surely that is religious Luddism – trying to cling to the security of the past by denying the reality of the present. An appreciation of history is essential for a healthy future, but our eyes must be forward-focused because that is the only direction of travel.

If the premise of this book is correct – that there is a wealth of information waiting to be read in our DNA – such information does not necessarily replace any existing scriptures, but it does predate all of them. By several billion years!

What might the message contain?

The Earth has more humans than it can realistically accommodate. At the time of writing there were just over 7.2 billion souls across the globe. During the 20th century the population in the world grew from 1.65 billion to 6 billion – and since 1970 the number of people in the world has doubled. According to the most recent United Nations estimates, the population of the world is expected to reach 8 billion people in the spring of 2024.

This is more than our resources can possibly maintain, at a time when supplies of energy and even food are falling behind increasing demand. And our sense of purpose, of direction, has become lost in most parts of the world, from the West to the Muslim world.

Perhaps we are at the point where the Earth and humans (as the pinnacle of life on the planet) need a full-blown reconnection with the creator – with God.

Many, perhaps most, world religions have lost contact with the masses – and even the once-great religions have fractured into an increasing number of sub-groups. The power blocs within some religions have lost the essence of their past and retained only the husk rather than the inner seed of their value. At the same time modern communications and travel possibilities have ensured that those who want to can inflict their inadequate insights onto the real world with thoughtless violence.

Whilst there has been a rise in the idea of the secular state, many countries, including the USA, seem unwilling to remove some notion of God from their politics. The USA is constitutionally committed to the separation of church and state, yet some 41 per cent of Americans attend weekly church services, as opposed to 10 per cent of Britons or 7.5

per cent of Australians. An even higher figure – 74 per cent–of Americans say they believe in God (though this is down from 82 per cent some years ago). In the United Kingdom, the Queen remains the head of the Church of England and recent prime ministers have publicly declared that God is central to their actions and claims of decency. Shockingly for a modern European country, even the action of going to war was justified by a prime minister in the name of God!

One of the most influential churchmen of recent times, Cardinal Carlo Martini of Milan, died on 31 August 2012. A renowned academic and biblical scholar, who was once strongly tipped as a future pope, Martini was also known to the leaders of other religions as a man who built bridges for mutual advantage.

After his death was announced, Jews, Muslims, Hindus and others expressed a sense of loss. He was a man who looked towards people... and the future rather than just the past. It seemed he was wise enough to see the past and the future as two sides of the same coin – spinning in front of his eyes. Knowing that his time was coming to an end, he provided an interview to be published after his death that has rocked the Roman Catholic establishment. He asked that his Church recognize that it was stuck 200 years in the past in an era that no longer existed. His parting words urged the Church to recognize its errors and to embark on a radical path of change – beginning with the pope. He said: 'Our culture has grown old, our churches are big and empty and the church bureaucracy rises up, our religious rites and the vestments we wear are pompous.' He urged a 'radical transition'.

Transition? Perhaps it is a failure to transit with the normal movement of time that has left so many religious institutions looking wooden, disconnected and ill informed. But maybe the great religions of the world have become overly wrapped up in their past and their ritual, sacrificing the energy and wisdom that once made them great for the eras that spawned them.

At the beginning of history the priests and the scientists were one and the same. The first and greatest science was observational astronomy, and the earliest religions were based on this and other sciences. The shift of power to kings, pharaohs and politicians tended to usurp the wisdom of the original – the real – priesthood. I suspect that the lure of magic and ritual in pursuit of the afterlife overtook the exercise of reason thousands of years ago.

In the 21st century, research tells us that most scientists do not reject God. At the same time ordinary people are turning their backs on religion all across the world, but particularly in the West.

## What if?

What if there was some greater knowledge possessed by the ancient prophets that has been lost down the road of time? What if there is a way to find our way again? Maybe information inside DNA that can be revealed by the mathematical values from the Earth, Moon and Sun. These could be the key to a new future where God – the creator of the universe – explicitly addresses us.

The evidence says that we are being addressed by God. And if there is even a small chance that the key to a DNA message is available, it must be investigated.

Life could be about to get more special. Humankind might just be about to leave the age of the child and enter a new period of maturity. Adult and mature, we, with God at our side, may be ready to enter a new age of reason and well-being.

# Chapter 14

# BEYOND COMMON SENSE

'To be too conscious is an illness.
A real thoroughgoing illness.'

*Fyodor Dostoyevsky*

Life is continually surprising. Those who outgrow the awe of childhood are diminished by their very maturity. Stunted by their logic and captive to the boundaries of reason.

How could it be that Stone Age builders designed and constructed complex structures using stones weighing many tons that were perfectly placed – to an accuracy of a hair's width? How come they used units of measurement that harmonize not only with the detailed physical characteristics of planet Earth, but also the Sun and the Moon?

Logic suggests to us that they could not have done these things. Who can blame the workaday archaeologists who will not even take the time to understand Alexander Thom's findings concerning the nature of Neolithic architecture?

Yet the science says the Neolithic builders did. So the awkward question remains and begs an answer.

Some years ago I read a piece in the journal *New Scientist*. It is a magazine that crosses the gap between stuffy and readable by being academically responsible and yet accessible to interested members of the public. Its staff writers are a little prone to intellectual woodenness but the work they report is invariably fascinating. The words that stood out were submitted by an engineer in Northern Ireland who was raising the subject of unreasonable expectations of archaeologists concerning the preservation of biological and manufactured materials buried in the ground. Jim Russell pointed out that if there had been a reasonably sophisticated civilization in the more distant past, we cannot expect to see anything of it today. Jim is a Chartered Civil Engineer working in concrete and steel design, specializing in piled foundations, with several patents to his name.

I contacted Jim and had a long telephone conversation during which it became clear that he was a no-nonsense kind of guy who was driven by practical outcomes. He had no particular interest in archaeology but was annoyed at the idea that an absence of artefact evidence means a great deal when talking about 5,000 or 10,000 years of being buried in the wet and windy British Isles. Whilst human remains can be desiccated and preserved for huge periods of time in the desert sands of Egypt, for example, they rot away rather quickly in damp, biologically rich soil.

Jim was very interested to hear about my work on Megalithic structures, humbly following in the footsteps of Professor Alexander Thom. He was especially taken by the idea that these people used stars to measure the Earth. He has since designed and built quite massive pieces of mobile equipment to reconstruct how the Neolithic astronomers could have measured the Earth with the technology of their age. In January 2014 Jim presented a paper at the Experimental Archaeology Conference at the University of Oxford on his refined Earth circumference method. This brought to life the methodology that Alan Butler and I had described. Jim demonstrated to the satisfaction of his audience how the Stone Age builder could have come to know the circumference of the Earth.

Several years ago Alan Butler and I invited Jim Russell to join us looking at a number of prehistoric henges and other Megalithic sites in Yorkshire that we had identified as being star-tracking and measuring equipment. Jim was thoughtful and as he looked up to the sky he said, 'Why would they not have known the world was round?'

Despite his matter-of-fact, bluff manner, Jim has a reflective and quick-moving mind. I was somewhat taken aback by a comment that Jim made as I dropped him back at the airport for his flight back to Belfast. He said, 'I don't know what those Megalithic builders were doing – but whatever it was, I've got the feeling that it is something extremely big and very, very different to anything we can imagine.' He paused before saying: 'It really is quite frightening.'

He was most serious and I could only nod in agreement.

What I had not told him was that I had particularly good reason to concur. I had had first-hand experience of a more illuminating, more terrifying side of Megalithic technology. I have written several books since my strange experience, but I have never described what happened to me on a windy hilltop some 15 years ago.

The reason I have previously refused to publish any part of what occurred on that occasion is that I could not begin to explain it. But now I believe I am starting to understand.

# The power of the stones

Before describing the events of that day back at the end of the 20th century, I have to state that I am a natural sceptic. I do not believe in anything easily and I despair (rightly or wrongly) of people who swing crystals, those who make ridiculous claims for obviously manmade crop circles and those who believe that aliens are walking among us. The reason I have never had religion is that I need evidence, not disembodied belief.

Now, on this particular day, my colleague and I were investigating a Megalithic structure with huge rows of relatively small stones aligned end to end. We knew that the ancient builders had frequently heated the stones to great temperatures, using piles of animal fat and bones, so that the stones could reach what is known as their Curie Temperature. This is the critical point where a material's intrinsic magnetic moments change direction. Magnetic moments are permanent dipole moments within the atom, which originate from an electron's angular momentum and spin. Materials have different structures of intrinsic magnetic moments that depend on temperature. At a material's Curie Temperature, those intrinsic magnetic moments change direction.

This means that the material within quartz crystals that make up the stone have a north and south magnetic pole themselves (like the planet itself). The alignment of these tiny magnetic entities is normally set in a chaotic state, where they face in all directions. However, there is reason to believe that the Megalithic builders heated these stones up to the point where the dipoles became free to move and potentially realign themselves. These Stone Age men then manoeuvred the slab-shaped stones so that they lay north to south within the Earth's magnetic field. This caused all of the dipoles within each stone to point in the same direction – to the poles of Earth's magnetic field.

As the stones cool, the dipoles remain permanently aligned and the stones can be placed in rows – creating a huge standing field of cohesive magnetism. This does not decay with time.

Many of the stones had been taken by roadbuilders centuries earlier, but most remained in place. What was amazing was that, as my colleague and I walked across the field of low stones – arranged like tombstones – it had a strange effect on our mobile phones. The rows were only a stride apart but as we stood on any row both phones showed zero signal. Half a step forward to stand in between a row and both phones showed maximum signal. Yet there was no phone service in the area at all.

Our mobile phones were picking up the discrete lines of magnetic force laid down before history began!

It did not take too long to identify the focal point of all these lines of magnetism. There was one spot, that was awkward to get to – that was THE SPOT.

Being dismissive of fanciful ideas, I readily volunteered to wander down and place myself at this focal point, which was on slightly lower ground than the curving army of stones. My colleague went to sit down on the other side of the little hill and I waited to see what might happen to me.

I expected that absolutely nothing would happen. I could not have been more wrong!

It was on a grey, overcast day that I stood and faced the stone rows with my eyes closed. The first thing I became aware of was a rushing, like fast-moving water around my head and shoulders. It was as though I was putting my hand to my face and dragging my hands forcefully backwards over my face and hair. It was powerful.

I realized it was like static electricity moving quickly across the top of my body, but I was already transfixed by the calm caused by what I saw. My eyes were closed but I could see a vibrant and perfect blue – like looking at a cloudless brilliant sky, or a TV set broadcasting just one colour.

The effect on me was soporific. I lost my sense of time and any purpose. I was relaxed and feeling extremely peaceful. I had the impression that something was missing, something else should have happened or might happen next.

It was about ten minutes later that my colleague walked forward and started shouting at me to stop. I didn't hear him, but a little later I just walked away – still peacefully relaxed.

As I got back into my car I was very aware that my head was pulsating – throbbing as though it was emitting waves of light or energy, like a flashing light. It was not a comfortable feeling. And I began to fear that I may have done some permanent damage to my head and perhaps my brain.

The pulsating effect continued all day and all night, and into the next day.

We decided to conduct a number of tests to see what, if anything, had changed about me. The crunch came when my colleague tried out some psychic tests. They were not exactly scientific, but they were real, and there was no room for any mistakes.

My colleague sat several feet behind me as I faced the other way with my eyes closed. We did not use the standard set of five Zener cards (circle, plus cross, wavy lines, square and star), which are designed to establish small deviations to chance.

I was responding to one-off original drawing being created behind my back. For example, my friend drew a shape and asked me what I had seen through my tightly closed eyes.

I replied: 'A keyhole.'

'Draw it,' said my colleague.

He then told me that he had drawn an orchestral triangle hanging from a holding ring. Side by side they looked the same.

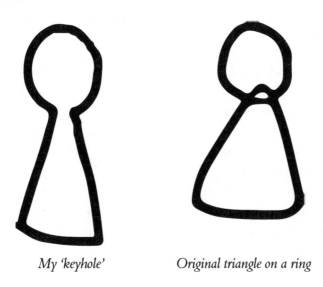

My 'keyhole'          Original triangle on a ring

Other tests followed, with the same result: I was psychic.

On one of these tests my colleague asked me what I had received and I said a pair of horns. I drew it and then he showed me the donkey he had drawn, rather badly. He had drawn the ears first and then hesitated for around ten seconds, trying to think how to draw the rest of the animal. It appears that I picked up the first thought but not the second.

The ability to draw things I could not see faded with the pulsating feeling that surrounded my head. Thank goodness.

Later, I spoke with a professor of particle physics who confirmed that the story sounded plausible in terms of the stones and their magnetic output. He was slightly surprised that our mobile phones had picked it up, but put that down to good fortune, as it was not difficult to understand.

I also told Professor Karl Pribram, the expert on the brain, about it and he was interested but not at all surprised at the strange effect that such a focused magnetic field could have had upon my grey matter.

## Towards a conclusion

We all see, smell, taste, touch and hear the world around us, and then our minds, consciously and unconsciously, create realities based on what our senses tell us. We generally believe that we are experiencing all there is to perceive, and we make assumptions based upon those perceptions, which ultimately shape our actions, world-view and ideologies.

Our brains have to work hard. The grey, ridged organ inside your cranium represents 3 per cent of the body's weight yet it consumes 20 per cent of your body's energy.

Without our senses, we could not understand the world around us, although human beings possess higher reasoning than anything else in the universe. But could it be that our reality may actually be a limited, perhaps even an illusory, perception?

When individual senses are directly compared to other animals, we look primitive in comparison. In fact, there is an entirely different reality being experienced by amphibians, fish, mammals, birds, insects and reptiles. These enhanced senses undoubtedly shape an entirely unique perception of existence for these animals.

We humans place a lot of emphasis on feelings, and understandably we seek out positive sensations – usually of love and harmony. Whilst the heart has always been the poetic seat of love within the human frame, we now know it is centred in or around the brain.

In Fyodor Dostoyevsky's novel *The Idiot*, Prince Myshkin experiences repeated epileptic seizures, accompanied by 'an incredible hitherto unsuspected feeling of bliss and appeasement', so that: 'All my problems, doubts and worries resolved themselves in a limpid subtle peace, with a feeling of understanding and awareness of the "Supreme Principle of life".'

At the University Hospital of Geneva a neurologist by the name of Fabienne Picard has spent years observing this very rare phenomenon that previous scientific literature has hardly noticed. Dr Picard acknowledges that the Russian author Dostoyevsky was the first to describe the effects that she has witnessed concerning ecstatic seizures experienced by some epileptic people. Those affected describe an incredibly intense feeling of well-being – as one of Picard's patients explains: 'During the seizure it is as if I were very, very conscious, more aware, and the sensations, everything seems bigger, overwhelming me.'

A Spanish architect observed by Picard reported the common sensation of some heightened connectedness. 'You are just feeling energy and all your senses… you take in everything that is around you. You get fusion.' Another patient, a 64-year-old woman, told *New Scientist* magazine: 'The immense joy that fills me is above physical sensations. It is a feeling of total presence, an absolute integration of myself, a felling of unbelievable harmony of my whole body and myself with life, with the world, with the all.'

Ecstatic seizures are not simply physically pleasurable, they also can cause an increased vividness of sensory perceptions, heightened feelings of self-awareness – of 'fitting' in the world – a feeling of time standing still, and a clarity of mind where all things suddenly fall into place, making perfect sense of everything. For some people this clarity involves a realization that some 'higher power' is responsible – even for atheists.

Such feelings of ecstasy, oneness with the world and a 'higher power' sound very much like the emotional response to the highest level of religious rapture. Indeed, many academics have argued that the descriptions given in the New Testament suggest a neurological origin for St Paul's ecstatic visions. Paul's physical state at the time of his conversion are said by some to be manifestations of temporal lobe epilepsy.*

'What I hear the most in my patients' stories', Picard is reported as saying, 'is a feeling of fullness, consistency, time dilation, mental clarity and the total absence of doubt. They tell me that they've never experienced anything better, so powerful. It sounds like a huge eureka!'

## The power of magnetism

Dr Jason J Braithwaite, a lecturer in cognitive psychology and brain science at the Behavioural Brain Sciences Centre, University of Birmingham, has been published widely in international, peer-reviewed journals. His field is visual cognition and its relationship to consciousness and awareness, hallucinations and anomalous cognition.

He notes that in recent years findings from a number of laboratory studies have suggested that anomalous, hallucinatory, haunt-type experiences can be artificially induced by applying temporally complex, weak-intensity magnetic fields to the outer cortex of the brain. Braithwaite and his colleagues also developed a 'magnetic anomaly detection system' to investigate anomalous magnetic fields associated with reputedly haunted locations.†

---

* Landsborough, D, 'St Paul and Temporal Lobe Epilepsy', *Journal of Neurology, Neurosurgery & Psychiatry*, June 1987, vol 50, no 6, pp 659–64

† Braithwaite J J, 'Magnetic Fields, Hallucinations and Anomalous Experiences: A sceptical critique of the current evidence', *The Skeptic*, 2009, vol 22, no 4, pp 38–45

He concluded that if the current evidence is to be accepted and future evidence supports it, then it appears there is an effect to be explained, albeit a subtle and somewhat nebulous one. At the very least the current evidence appears sufficient to warrant considerable further investigation. If the effects on behaviour and experience are reliable then they implicate some form of non-induction-based coupling mechanism between a weak complex magnetic field and the human brain.

I recall at this point how Karl Pribram suggested that if we humans were deprived of our 'normal' sensory receptors, we would become immersed in holographic experiences.

I said earlier that this profound concept might explain a great deal about our past – and potentially shape our future.

Have our senses become too oriented to the straight, two-dimensional line we take to be reality? Has the maturity of our civilization cost us some aspect of our souls? Are we blinded by the light and deafened by the cacophony of sounds that surround us? And can we find a way back in time – through science?

I have come to believe that Jim Russell's gut reaction to the Megalithic structures was right. The people who erected these stones had a means of connecting with the world that we have absolutely forgotten.

How did these prehistoric people know how to measure the Earth, and how did they construct units of measure that arise out the very heartbeat of our Sun–Moon–Earth system? The first answer is that they were very intelligent engineers, but they also knew how to close their eyes and sense the world. Something beyond seeing, hearing, touching, tasting and smelling it.

And possibly the reason we have not had a great religious leader emerge since the time of Muhammad is because we have all lost our ability to connect with the greater, but unseen, order of things.

With over 7.2 billion people on the planet and resources running thin, maybe it is time to look up to the heavens and notice (as our distant forebears did) that the patterns of the Sun and Moon dance in tune to our blue Earth. There is a design here that did not arise out of chaos. That design is talking to us and telling us to pay attention.

We have eyes to see – let us hope that there are enough voices in the academic and political establishment to proclaim that what our eyes are telling us is almost certainly the tip of a greater insight. One that we have seen before – yet now forgotten.

The pound weight, the pint, the yard and mile live on, as does the litre, metre and the second of time. These units are super-ancient ones but have somehow survived – possibly because they are truly aspects of 'the great reality' of which we are a vital part.

We need to better understand the way that the Megalithic builders thought and we need to investigate their 'spiritual technology'. But, unlike the madness of the Taliban, we do not have to revert to living in history in order to build a future that works with rather than against the Creator.

Some strange and distant science underpinned the work-ings of the Neolithic mind as they super-heated stones to build up coherent magnetic landscapes that took their priesthood to places we cannot fathom. They engineered wonders with the simplest of tools and they measured the movement of the planet as it spun through the year around its mother star.

We have a different science, but we share the same wonder and the same need to understand – and to connect.

Most scientists either embrace the idea of a God or they have failed to be able to dismiss it. If the evidence points towards a creator we must not be afraid to change our minds and embrace the new reality. Anthony Flew has shown us the way by his fearless willingness to turn a hard-fought-for lifetime's work on its head when the facts changed. We must follow Anthony Flew's shining example.

If DNA might hold a message from the beginning of time, as some leading academics have suggested, we must investigate. If the world wakes up to the magical mathematical patterning built into our Earth and its Sun and Moon, we must look deeper and think harder – in a softer way!

# Appendix

# THE CREATOR GOD OF RELIGION

When we speak of the power or mind that designed and built the universe, placed DNA in all living beings, made human beings the pinnacle of creation and set the size and movements of the Earth, Moon and Sun in a mathematically ordered pattern, we call this creator 'God'. This is a term familiar to us from most religions and translated into all human languages. God, Allah, YHWH, Deus, Khoda, Khodavand, Adoshem, El, Elohim, El Shaddai, Adonai, Elyon, Avinu, Baali, dozens more descriptive terms in Judaism, the '99 Most Beautiful Names of God' in Islam, the 101 names in Zoroastrianism, and many more in ancient and modern religions alike. All signify the creator of the universe, a being above all other beings – who is almighty, transcendent, all-knowing, all-powerful, all-compassionate, all-hearing, all-seeing, unique, eternal, without beginning or end – yet, in Quranic terms, 'closer to man than his jugular vein'.*

The creator God, this great designer, causes a sense of duality in most religions. In the words of the famous Jewish

---

* Quran 50.16

203

declaration known as the Shema, recited during the morning and evening prayers: *Shema Yisrael Adonai eloheinu Adonai Ehad* ('Hear O Israel, the Lord is our God, the Lord is One'). The singularity of God was passed by the Jews into all other forms of monotheism. In Islam, the first of the prayer-summoners (*mu'adhin*) was an Ethiopian called Bilal al-Habashi. When he first converted to the new faith, his owners (he was a slave) subjected him to various forms of torture, but as they dragged him round the streets of Mecca, he recited the words '*Ahad, Ahad*' ('One, One'), meaning that God is one. Part of the Islamic declaration of faith (also used in the call to prayer) is '*La ilaha illa'llah*' ('There is no god but God'). The Quran condemns the Christian belief in the Trinity as a form of polytheism, regardless of attempts by Christian theologians to explain that the three persons of the Trinity merge as a single God.

No religion has produced a more extensive – and complicated – system of divine representation than Hinduism, in which an almost endless succession of sects and philosophical schools have weaved a network of worship and scriptural density in which a single creative power is manifested in numerous spiritual and material forms. In Vaishnavism, we find the earliest form of Hindu monotheism. The Supreme Being takes two forms, Vishnu and Narayana, who have many avatars, chief among whom is Krishna. In another version, the god Krishna himself is 'the original Personality of Godhead'. His title is Svayam Bhagavan ('the Lord Himself'), and is used to show him as the Supreme Lord and the source of all incarnations.

The important Smarta philosophy allows Hindus to venerate numerous deities, but only on the understanding that they are all just manifestations of one divine power.

The Trimurti concept comes closest to the Christian idea of the Trinity by postulating three gods – Brahma the creator, Vishnu the preserver and Shiva the destroyer – as manifestations of one person, the almighty Parabrahman, or Supreme Being.

Brahma is the nearest thing in Hinduism to the single God of the Abrahamic religions. He is referred to as the Absolute, the Godhead which encompasses all matter, energy, time, space, being – everything in and beyond this universe. He can be perceived as either personal or impersonal.

This duality between an impersonal superbeing and a personal God typifies a dilemma for the monotheistic religion. If human beings are going to worship a divinity, it is hard to do so if it is an abstract entity beyond human understanding. And it's not simply worship, it's the formation of a close relationship with a person with whom one may talk, to whom one can be faithful, whom one can love almost as one loves a human being.

In some religions, God is closer than that jugular vein. In Christianity, believers can partake of God's body and blood in the Mass. This ingestion of the divine brings the believer into an intimate relationship with God through the person of Jesus Christ, the most human aspect of the Trinity. Jesus' most important characteristic is his humanity, in that he was born of a human mother, raised as a human child and underwent appalling suffering and died as a mortal man.

Other religions use similar methods to serve as a bridge between the transcendent creator and the human realm. Although orthodox Islam disavows all that detracts from God's unapproachability, both Sufi and Shi'i Islam have created a very different perspective.

In Sufism, formal worship (the five-times-a-day *salat*) is supplemented by gatherings of each of the many orders or brotherhoods. This chiefly takes the form of chanting in a *hadra*, or 'circle'. This ritual is known as *dhikr*, or 'remembrance' – that is to say, remembrance of God – and it brings the divine down to a human level. Sufi orders are led by a *shaykh* (an 'elder') or *murshid* ('guide'), a man whose erudition and spiritual training give him the status of one who links his followers to God, not unlike the role of a *guru* in Hinduism. Brotherhoods (which are fewer today than in the past) retain a local habitation and a name in their 'meeting-places' or *khanqah*s. The shrines of dead saints (or of a succession of father-to-son *shaykh*s) become sites for pilgrimage (*ziyara*, as distinct from the better-known *hajj* to Mecca), particularly in North Africa and the Indian subcontinent.

Similar shrines exist in Shi'i Islam, notably in Iraq and Iran. Shi'ism is built around a succession of holy figures, the 12 *imam*s, beginning with Muhammad's son-in-law 'Ali and his two sons Hasan and Husayn, followed by their direct descendants. The great French scholar Henry Corbin wrote a four-volume study of the metaphysics of Twelver Shi'ism, in which he shows how the *imam*s, alongside Muhammad's daughter Fatima, function as intermediaries between the divine and human realms. This sense of transcendence brought down to the human plane is particularly noted in a form of Shi'i theophany called the Ishraqi or Illuminationist philosophy. This scheme of looking at the world originated with Shihab al-Din Yahya Suhrawardi (1155–91), an Iranian mystic who was executed for heresy. It was later expanded by several Shi'i thinkers during the 16th to 19th centuries, notably Mulla

Sadra Shirazi (1572–1640), who has been claimed as the most important and influential thinker in the Islamic world in the last 400 years. The School of Isfahan that was built around Illuminationist philosophy was the most important intellectual movement in Islam for several centuries, taking Shi'ism well beyond the majority Sunni world as a repository of both Islamic and ancient wisdom.

Despite its near collapse by the end of the 19th century, many of the concepts of the Ishraqi school came down to influence a new religion, Baha'ism, which consciously moved away from Islam. There are now between 5 and 7 million followers of Baha'ism around the world, though almost none in Islamic countries. A key concept of the faith is *mazhariyyat*, the quality of first-class prophets to appear as manifestations (*mazhar, mazahir*) of God. Thus, Abraham, Moses, Jesus, Muhammad and even Buddha and Krishna are all manifestations of God, to the extent that the Baha'i founder, Baha' Allah, claimed to be God on Earth. In Baha'i theology, the Supreme God cannot be described or understood, imagined or pictured. The same in Judaism, Islam and other forms of monotheism. Human beings are expected to worship him and are threatened with dire consequences if they do not.

But it is the manifestation that people focus on. When they want to worship, to look for blessings, to visit shrines on pilgrimage, to keep a sacred statue in their home, to light candles before a holy picture, to imagine a divinity who listens and sees, and perhaps even speaks to them, it is not the abstract God they turn to but the manifestation. Lord Krishna's picture on the family wall is an icon of God's presence. So are statuettes of the Crucifixion or the Virgin in a blue mantle. Stories of Jesus, Muhammad, the Bab or Guru Nanak bring the believer close to the divine in human form.

All this enables religions to function on the everyday level. But it is the personal God who causes most problems for mankind and makes it hard or impossible for believers to think of the vastnesses of space that we have been talking about. It is the personal God who governs His followers' behaviour. Don't drink alcohol, don't have sex outside marriage, stone the adulterer, hang the homosexual, keep yourselves apart from other people, fight holy wars against non-believers, wear phylacteries, don't permit abortions, do not use contraception, wear a veil, and so on.

These examples can be multiplied, but they show a negative side of religion. Sometimes they come directly from scripture, at other times they have their origin in the dicta of holy men or institutions such as the Vatican, the Baha'i Universal House of Justice, or the First Presidency and Quorum of the Twelve Apostles of the Mormon Church. A misplaced belief in the infallibility of their judgements tends to pass down through these institutions to the extent that any form of challenge to their authority is taken as a sign of heresy or apostasy.

Established religious leaders and institutions are always conservative. They need to prevent any overt tampering with the system they defend because it is likely to lead to precisely the sort of challenge to their authority that will, if unfettered, shake the foundations of the religion and belief in God himself. It is a dogma in Islam that every word and letter of the Quran is directly taken (via the angel Jibril [Gabriel]) from a heavenly tablet that bears God's unalloyed word. If anyone were to suggest a grammatical error, a misspelling, or the need for a different word here or there, it would open the floodgates. For, if one change can be made, perhaps the whole thing can be changed, or enough of it to deny its divine origin.

It is another Islamic dogma that all innovations are unbelief (*kullu bid'a kufr*). This is why Islamic civilization went backwards from about the 12th century. Before then, the Islamic world was ahead of the West or China in its science, philosophy and general intellectual output. After that there was no room for innovation, and today most Muslim countries remain seriously behind in science and economic development, as well as in social improvements such as human rights, equality of the sexes, tolerance towards homosexuals or religious minorities.

The Roman Catholic Church has led to similar (though lighter) forms of social stagnation. The ban on divorce has created a great deal of human unhappiness, whilst the prohibition on the use of condoms has resulted in many unwanted cases of AIDS in the Third World. Opposition to the ideas of Copernicus and Galileo blocked for some time the paradigm shift in astronomy that should have happened earlier. Nowadays, the dogmatic persistence of evangelical Christian groups opposed to the theory of evolution stunts many young minds and gives them the questionable liberty to think there is a better way of doing science (on the basis of the Bible).

The ideas put forward in this book are necessarily out of kilter with mainstream scientific opinion, and will be opposed as such. But just as Galileo had evidence for his heliocentric theories, so I have presented mathematical and other evidence that is adequate for the enquiring mind. Scientists have their particular issues with innovation. But theirs is not the greatest problem with my argument. The measurements we have presented are there for anyone else to calculate. The calendrical evidence we have presented has been known for centuries. The problem for scientists is what it usually is: how to come to terms with the idea of an all-powerful creator God. Now, many scientists do believe in God, not least those who live in places where belief in a deity is almost 100 per cent. For them, such a transition would not be problematic.

But hardline sceptics, for whom the idea of intelligent design or a Supreme Being is as absurd as a belief in fairies, trolls or witches, are congenitally creatures of doubt and they dislike the thought of going outside their scientific world-view every bit as much as dyed-in-the-wool believers repine even at the thought that another prophet might be true. Normally, there is little or no likelihood of someone deeply committed to a materialistic world-view coming to a belief in God. That's not surprising, given the absurdity of almost every religious belief. Stories of virgin births, of miracles, of God speaking from a burning bush, of weeping statues, of winged horses, of bodies raised from the dead, of angels dictating verses from a heavenly book – all such staples are stumbling blocks to true sceptics. More than anyone, scientists are trained to be sceptical – and rightly so, for science would not work without the ability to call certain things into question. It may look as if the Sun goes round the Earth, but the good sceptic will make some mathematical calculations and prove that it does not. On the basis of those and later calculations, we have been able to send men to the Moon and probes to Jupiter and beyond.

# INDEX

211

Babi religion 82
Babylonians 84, 143
Baha' Allah 88, 161, 207
Baha'ism 88, 207
Balabanova, Svetla 75–6
*Before the Pyramids* 138
Bendeliani, N. A. 47
Berekaht Ram figurine 27
Berthelot, Marcellin 43
*bhutatmas* 29
Big Bang theory xx, 1, 13–17,
    18–19, 61
Bilal al-Hibashi 204
Black Death 52
Bodhidharma 82
*bodhisattvas* 82
Bohm, David 31
Bondi, Hermann 16
Book of Enoch 28
Boss, Alan 108, 109
Bradley, Bruce A. 53
Brahma 85, 205
brain
    age of modern 27
    chemical synthesis 72–3
    effect of magnetism 193–6,
        199–200
    effects of sensory deprivation 35
    holographic model 28–31
    and plant-derived drugs 75–7
    as seat of love 197
Braithwaite, Jason J 199–200
Bristol 50
Buddha 88, 178, 207
Buddhism 32, 82, 86
Butler, Alan xii–xiii, 116, 132, 136,
    138, 144, 147, 172, 191

Callanish ('Moon temple) 133
carbon 2, 38, 40, 70
    origins of 18–19
cars 39–42
'Casimir effect' 10
Catal Huyuk 83

Celsius, Andrei 122
CERN Large Hadron Collider 146
Charles, Prince of Wales 74
chemistry 45, 67, 90
Chesterton, G. K. 115
China, creation myths 85
Chinese Folk Religions 86
Christianity xviii, 56, 87, 89, 160,
    161, 178, 204, 205
    Dawkins' denouncement 59
    new forms 90
    opposition to evolution theory
        xx, 58, 92, 209
    polytheistic elements 82, 83
    prevalence 56, 86
chromosomes 172
Church, George 180
*Civilization One* 138, 144
Clovis culture 53
cocaine 75
Cocconi, Giuseppe 163
Cold War 170
Columbus, Christopher 49, 50,
    53, 54
comets 105–6
Conan Doyle, Arthur 150–1
Condamine, Charles Marie de La
    42
Copernican principle 157
Copernicus, Nicholas 4, 92, 157,
    209
Corbin, Henry 206
cosmology 14, 159
creation 13–20
    as an accident 17–20
    definition xix–xx
    God and 13, 56, 154–6, 160
    as ongoing process 10
    religious accounts xx, 58
    *see also* Big Bang theory;
        intelligent design; Steady
        State theory
creation myths 83–6
'Creationism' 58

medicine 8–9, 24, 71–2
Megalithic degrees of arc 137, 138,
    151, 152–4, 155
Megalithic seconds of arc 118, 119,
    121, 122, 138
Megalithic structures/henges
    132–7, 144, 149, 189, 190–1,
    200, 201
    astronomical alignments 133,
        152–4
    power of 192–6
Megalithic Yard 132, 133–4, 136–7,
    138, 144, 146, 181
meditation 35
memory, holographic model
    29–31
Mendeleev, Dmitri 43
Mercury 94, 102, 104
metal 40
methane 46, 96
Methodism 90
meteors 103–4
metre, ancient 142
metric system 116, 119–20, 129
    ancient 143–5, 147
metron 119, 127, 128, 129, 134
Middle East oil reserves 46–7
Milky Way 92, 164
Miller, Stanley L. 174
Miller, Jonathan 8–9
Minoan culture xiii, 132, 138
Minoan Foot 132, 138
mitochondria 68
molecular biology 67
monotheism 81–2, 204–5, 207
    imaginary distinction with
        polytheism 83
Moon 85, 181–2
    alignment with henges 133,
        152–4
    appears same size as the Sun
        119, 151, 155
    circumference 117, 119, 149,
        151–2

expansion of orbit over time
    167–8
gravitational pull 101
lack of water 104
as message 166–71
meteorite craters 103
as planetary stabilizer 102,
    181–2
relationship with Sun and Earth
    xiii, 151–4, 156, 166–9,
    170–1, 181–2, 201, 202
rotation rate 100
temperature 96
*see also* EMS measurement
    system
Mora, Peter T. 173
morphine 72
Morrison, Phillip 163
Muhammad 87, 160, 178, 208
Mulla Sadra Shirazi 207
musical frequencies 122–3
Mutually Assured Destruction
    (MAD) 170
mysticism, definition xviii

NASA 106, 108, 119, 158, 161
Nasir al-Din Shah 57
Native American stone calendars
    135
natural selection 61, 90
*Nature* 69, 163
Neanderthals 68–9
Neolithic (Stone Age) peoples
    132–8, 167, 189, 190–1, 201
    standard view 145, 146–7
    unlikelihood of mapping the
        Sun and Moon 150, 151
*Nepenthes* pitcher plants 70
Neptune 94, 106
neutrons 6, 19, 39
*New Scientist* 165, 190, 189
Newbegin, Hilary xiii
Newton, Isaac 17, 58
NGC 4319 16

# Index

# Index

Kepler 22b 108–9
measurement 121–2
Moon 96
Venus 97
theology xiv, 20, 23, 81
and science 91
Thom, Alexander 132–6, 138, 144,
189, 190
Tibetan Buddhism 82
Titan 96–7
Toltec People 52
tomato plants 74
Transcutaneous Electrical Nerve
Stimulation (TENS)
machines 72
Travolta, John 24
Trinkhaus, Eric 68
tsunami (2004) 32–3
*tzadiks* 82

Ubaidians 143
universe
age of 38–9
composition 158–9
expansion 15, 158
homogeneic and isotropic
assumption 157
*Upanishads* 29
Uranus 94, 99–100, 106
*Uriel's Machine* xiii
Ussher, Archbishop 58

Vaishnavism 204
*Vedas* 29
Venter, Craig 178–9
Venus 54, 94, 97, 104, 109
*la merica* 54
as measuring aid 126, 129, 138
Venus flytrap 70
Vespucci, Amerigo 54
Virgin Mary 83, 208
virtual particles 10
Vishnu 85, 204, 205
von Neumann, John 31

Waldseemüller, Martin 54
water 95
on Earth 98–9
meteors as Earth's source
103–4
Watson, Lyall 173
Whewell, William 7
Wilkinson Microwave Anistrophy
Probe (WMAP) 158–9
Williams, Rowan 59
Wilson, Chris 10
Wright, Gregory 165–6

Xenu 23, 24

Yahweh 86, 87, 178

Zen Buddhism 82

# WATKINS

Sharing Wisdom Since
1893

The story of Watkins Publishing dates back to March 1893, when John M. Watkins, a scholar of esotericism, overheard his friend and teacher Madame Blavatsky lamenting the fact that there was nowhere in London to buy books on mysticism, occultism or metaphysics. At that moment Watkins was born, soon to become the home of many of the leading lights of spiritual literature, including Carl Jung, Rudolf Steiner, Alice Bailey and Chögyam Trungpa.

Today our passion for vigorous questioning is still resolute. With over 350 titles on our list, Watkins Publishing reflects the development of spiritual thinking and new science over the past 120 years. We remain at the cutting edge, committed to publishing books that change lives.

## DISCOVER MORE ...

Read our blog

Watch and listen to
our authors in action

Sign up to
our mailing list

## JOIN IN THE CONVERSATION

f WatkinsPublishing        🐦 @watkinswisdom

▶ WatkinsPublishingLtd     8+ +watkinspublishing1893

Our books celebrate conscious, passionate, wise and happy living.
Be part of the community by visiting

www.watkinspublishing.com